*Writing and Selling
the Romance Novel*

♥ Writing and Selling the Romance Novel

Edited by

SYLVIA K. BURACK

BOSTON
THE WRITER, INC.
PUBLISHERS

Library of Congress Cataloging in Publication Data

Main entry under title:
Writing and selling the romance novel.

1. Love stories—Authorship.   I. Burack, Sylvia K.
PN3377.5.L68W7   1983   808′.02   83-6859
ISBN 0-87116-134-6 (pbk.)

Printed in the United States of America

Contents

Foreword

In spite of the talk of doom and gloom about publishing that appears almost daily in the press, there is an upbeat side: the romance novel field. With sales of romance novels (published primarily in paperback) reaching an estimated $250 million in the past year and expected to increase over the next several years to level off at approximately $500 million, it's no wonder that there is an almost frenetic competition among editors of romance novels and their parent publishing houses to acquire authors and come up with intriguing labels for new romance lines.

From the point of view of the fiction writer willing to move in the direction of the romance novel, the situation couldn't be more inviting. There is in fact no other field in publishing today that is so eager for the work of new writers. Where else in book publishing will editors court never-before-published novelists, often simply on the basis of a letter, sometimes a sample chapter and synopsis; where big-name writers don't really have any special advantage, since the vast majority of romance novels are published under pseudonyms? What other field publishes 100 new titles a month, ranging from the contemporary romance, the Regency, the Gothic, and the historical to teen-age or young adult, Christian, ethnic, problem romance, and romantic suspense? (The shelf life of a romance novel is short, hence the constant need for new titles.) All a writer needs is talent, and a feel and flair for romance. The novels can take place in the high-geared world of today's career-minded but always romantic heroine, or in the 18th or 19th century or Victorian world of the repressed but passionate young woman seeking to escape the strictures of her life.

Though editors of most romance lines supply guidelines (sometimes called "tip sheets") to help aspiring novelists write within a rather broad romance novel framework, there is ample room for the writer to express her (most but not all romance novelists are women) originality, point of view, imagination, and preferences in creating the heroine, hero, villain, setting, plot, degree of sensuality and sexuality, and explicit or implied sexual encounters. Each romance line has its own special requirements (and even biases) described in detail in the tip sheets, where available. For instance, one line might indicate a preference for strong heroines, rather than the simple-minded, clinging vines; some lines are "wholesome" while others specify explicit sex scenes—erotic and sensual, though "always in good taste"; some want young heroines with heroes from three to six years older than they; and the romance novels with "mature" heroines seek male romantic "leads" who are successful and dominant in their work, but vulnerable in their romantic lives, many with problems they can't seem to master or solve without the help of the middle-aged heroine. Guidelines also include information on word length, setting, whether the editors want completed manuscripts, queries with sample chapters, synopses and outlines, and many other details to help the writer shape and direct her manuscript toward a particular line.

A careful examination of the current trends reveals that the overwhelming number of romance novels now being published are contemporary adult romances: 41–50% of today's paperback sales are romance novels, and two-thirds of those are the contemporary romances. Not only is there an ever-increasing demand for manuscripts to meet the publishers' needs, but the requirements are constantly changing, sometimes slightly, sometimes quite radically, to more sex, longer word lengths (now up to 100,000 words); more sensual descriptions, and more sophisticated settings; maturer themes (though *never* abortion or birth control); less dominant males (though always magnetic and attractive if not physically handsome).

Heroines are older (26 and up), possibly reflecting the present trend for women to marry in their late twenties and early thirties—a situation true to life and easy for readers to identify with. Endings tend to be "happy," but not in the inane way that characterized romances of the 1930s, with their unfailing "lived happily ever after" endings. It is, however, interesting to note that some of the romance novels of that period by such writers as Emilie Loring and Grace Livingston Hill, for example, are being currently reissued (with newly designed, appropriately seductive covers).

Many of the heroines in these contemporary romances are successful career women, some divorced, widowed, and almost always "experienced," revealing the virtual disappearance of taboos about loss of virginity and similar proscriptions. Even when they are looking for "Mr. Right," a man who will be able to offer them romance and even take charge, the women are more assertive in the adult contemporary novels. They are independent, even aggressive, though not in an obnoxious way; they often "make the first move" in the relationship. And though marriage is not necessarily the inevitable goal, some kind of commitment is required. Unmarried alliances, for instance, are certainly common in these books, as are detailed descriptions of physical acts of love. As one editor put it, "mature men and women who are having a relationship do go to bed together."

But while the "sweet and wholesome" tradition in romantic novels is not as popular, there is still a demand by the publishers of the young adult and Christian romances for the more conventional romance, with the sweet heroine and the handsome hero who courts her in the traditional way, as they "walk off into the sunset together." New lines in these categories are being started by various publishers, and some are even sold through book clubs in the schools. The important message here is that even though *contemporary* romances outsell other categories by a wide margin, it may be that writers just trying to break into the romance novel field would find the large number of historical, young adult, romantic suspense, and Regency romance novels good places to begin.

A picture of romance novel readers can be very helpful to writers interested in entering this field, and much information is available not only in the guidelines published by romance novel publishers, but also in the dozens of articles that appear regularly in general magazines, book pages, and financial pages of such major newspapers as *The Wall Street Journal* and *The New York Times*.

There is no "typical" romance reader, but there are some broad general facts known: Most romance readers are women ranging in age from 18–60, with the concentration between 26 and 45. (Readers of teen-age and young adult romances are much younger, typically 10–16.) They are for the most part suburban working women, though a number of readers live in rural communities or small towns. They tend to live conventional lives and look to romance novels for relaxation or escape, for insight into problems or situations similar to those they have encountered—or would like to. According to a number of studies, romance novel readers spend as much as $25.00 a month or more on romance novels, often buying three or four at a time. These readers—many college-educated—want "things to come out right," as their heroines—and in fantasy, *they*—search for the perfect male lover or romantic hero.

A number of readers rely on their local libraries for "romantic escape." Public libraries across the country are buying and circulating romances from all the major publishers, and reports indicate that those libraries with romance collections rank very high in terms of circulation and community use. One library's collection began and continues with the help of romance-reading patrons who donate their own novels when they're through reading them.

It is readily understandable that such a vast field should not only have an immense impact on the readers and their families and friends (many publishers consider word-of-mouth the most important sales tool for romances), but would generate discussion, study, and controversy on every level. While many critics and observers of the literary scene trying to analyze the incredibly large readership and seemingly inexhaustible demand for new romances see them as harmless fantasies for women, and others as "sex manuals" not only for young adults but for older women, some take a darker view. They see the contemporary romances in particular as sexist, racist, insidious, exploitative, even titillating to the point of being almost pornographic. But like the centipede (who cannot tell which leg goes first), their popularity defies any one neat theory, and romance novels continue to sell by the tens of millions.

Romance writers are of all ages, typically from the mid-twenties to the mid-forties, and though almost all are women, there are a few successful men in the romance novel field—for example, Tom Huff, who writes very successfully under the pseudonym of Jennifer Wilde. And speaking of pseudonyms, most romance novels are written under pen names, often several assumed or assigned by an editor to a single author who may write up to six books or more a year, not only under different names, but for different imprints.

Some authors write in more than one genre of the category novel—contemporary as well as historical; teen-age or young adult along with Christian (both demand a level of "wholesome" writing not required in the other types). Whether an author aims for a modest sales record, or achieves the stunning record of novelist Janet Dailey, whose romances have topped 100 million copies, or of Barbara Cartland, with accumulated sales of her novels in the hundreds of millions, she can be sure that with talent and hard work she can produce manuscripts that will be assessed and sought after by knowledgeable editors, who read as many as 150 unsolicited romance manuscripts a month.

To keep author (and reader) interest at a high pitch of excitement, several organizations (including the Ro-

mance Writers of America and Romance Book Club)
have been formed, and regional as well as national conferences are held regularly, attracting large numbers of
big-name and prospective writers as well as fans of the
writers, who feed their fancies and fantasies. The promotion of these conferences is vigorous, with special
events, advance publicity, and newspaper articles, as
well as best-selling writers and the editors of the leading
romance novel series, as the main attractions. For example, the fan magazine *The Romantic Times* sponsored a
conference in New York, for which a "love train" actually crossed the country with a great deal of fanfare,
stopping for several hours or more at various cities en
route from California to New York.

There are all kinds of advertising and promotion
gimmicks used to keep information about romance
novels and the requirements of various publishers and
editors up-to-date: not only the magazines like *The
Writer*, in its Market News columns, but special publica-
tions like *The Love Line, Heart Lines, The Romantic Times,
Love Notes* (put out by Waldenbooks, one of the major
bookstore chains), and *Boy Meets Girl*, edited by a bookstore owner who keeps up to the minute with authors,
books, and shifts and changes of the market.

There is no other field of writing in which the publishers' efforts to "court" their readers go so far beyond the normal amount of advertising and promotion
that is part of all publishing. One romance novel publisher spends $20 million a year on TV commercials
alone to promote its books; another spent $7 million last
year on similar advertising. Other companies prefer to
concentrate on talk shows to interview romance editors
or best-selling authors. All of this is further enhanced
and sales bolstered for writers by local interviews and

autographing parties at bookstores or reading groups, drawing large numbers of fans and readers—one might even say "addicts." One of the large publishers holds "thank you" parties for readers in various places across the country, attracting hundreds of the faithful who come to meet authors, get samples, and get pep talks and firsthand behind-the-scenes views of their favorite reading matter—and then go off happily to buy and read more romance novels.

What does all of this mean to writers? A warm welcome for new and experienced writers, and editors who travel constantly to various cities and regions simply to attract new writers and offer them inducements to submit their manuscripts to a particular house.

Unlike the more standard kind of novel publishing, publication of romance novels is constantly changing, with some lines being dropped, new ones added, and still others changing their editorial requirements. It is therefore advisable, actually essential, for a writer to make sure that she has the most current needs and preferences for a particular line at the time she is submitting her manuscript. Writers should check with publishers on guidelines and tip sheets as issued and verify by letter (or request an updated tip sheet) just what an editor wants to see. There is no other way to be absolutely sure about an editor's needs at a specific time, since editors and publishers are very competitive and often keep information about the names of new lines or changes in old ones "under wraps" till the last possible minute.

That the romance novel has satisfied an enormous, widespread need in readers all over the country is unquestionable. The sales figures speak for themselves. And as long as that continues—and there is no sign that it will abate—there will be a need for more and better romance novel writers who are willing to master their craft, study the market, and work hard and persistently to achieve success in the receptive, booming romance novel field.

Special note: As in all fields of writing, there are many approaches, many techniques, and many styles that various romance writers have found to work best for them. Readers and prospective writers may find contradictory points of view and advice in this book, since no attempt has been made to endorse one method over any other.

S.K.B.

*Writing and Selling
the Romance Novel*

1

WRITING THE CATEGORY ROMANCE

by Barbara Delinsky

Pseudonyms:	Bonnie Drake
	Billie Douglass
Imprints:	Dell Candlelight Ecstasy
	Silhouette Special Edition
	Silhouette Desire

CATEGORY romance has come of age at last. In the past three years, when a stalling economy has put many other aspects of publishing on hold, the genre has thrived. What started as a field dominated by the Harlequin Romance has now expanded to include monthly entries by Dell, Simon and Schuster, Jove, Bantam, and New American Library, among others.

Why do readers flock by the millions to buy category romance? For one thing, they find romance novels shorter, easier to read, and therefore more pleasurable than some of the heavier fare on the bookstore shelves. New romance titles appear monthly, each a self-contained entertainment unit, a predictably good read. For another, the category romance is priced lower than most mainstream novels, and, finally, and most important, it offers a story of love and happiness, a story in which problems are met and resolved, a story in which two people discover, in their union, something far greater than the simple sum of their parts.

Sound trite? Or corny? Then, read no further! For the most fundamental prerequisite to writing romance is *loving* romance. It is the one element that unites romance writers with their readers, and it is inescapable.

My own entry into the field of romance novel writing was quite by accident. As opposed to many of my colleagues, I had not been a fan first. A romantic, yes; a regular reader of romance, no. Indeed, I was nearly ignorant of the field until I spotted a newspaper article on the category romance and its authors. Call it fate . . . or destiny . . . or a certain spark kindled in that instant— but something appealed to me at the thought of giving it a try.

Enthusiastically, if systematically, I pored over forty or fifty Harlequin Romances, outlined them with paper and pencil, tried to discern the much-touted "formula," then set out to write my own novel. After an intense three-and-a-half weeks of near-constant work, I sent off that first manuscript. Six weeks later, it was picked up from the slush pile and bought by Dell, who brought it out as *The Passionate Touch,* under the pseudonym Bonnie Drake. Less than three years after finishing that first romance novel, I mailed number twenty-one off to my editor in New York.

How does one go about writing category romance? First, one reads. One reads *widely.* One reads widely *in the field.* It is not enough to pick up one or two romances that were published even as recently as a year or two ago. The field is changing so rapidly that one must buy last month's books, *this* month's books to get an accurate glimpse of what is being bought now for publication next year. For category romance *is* different from the mainstream novel in that it stays within certain guidelines—ever-widening guidelines, but guidelines nonetheless. Which leads to the second step in writing romance—setting your eye on a market.

Identify the publishing houses that publish category romance and send for tip sheets. First and foremost, such tip sheets indicate the length of manuscript a particular house wants, a figure that varies from 50,000 to 100,000 words, depending on the line. Some imprints, such as Simon and Schuster's Silhouette, have multiple lines, each with its own length requirements and guidelines. Today, most category romances are in either a 188-page or a 256-page format, though this, too, may change.

Tip sheets suggest the preferred ages of hero and heroine (most commonly between 25 and 40); types of setting (some American, others European or "exotic"); and occupations (often professional, always interesting), plus the kinds of conflicts preferred for a given line— physical or emotional, internal or external. Tip sheets also indicate the acceptable level of sensuality, varying from sweet (as in a typical Silhouette Romance) to provocative (as in a Dell Ecstasy, a Silhouette Desire, an NAL Rapture, or a Bantam Loveswept). Finally, tip sheets list those taboos—such as violence, infidelity, and overwhelming tragedy—which, if included in your work, would guarantee a speedy rejection.

Much as these guidelines might be scoffed at, we who regularly write category romance respect them, just as we respect the hundreds of thousands of readers who inspire them. These readers are primarily women, as often married as single, with as many college and post-graduate degrees as high school diplomas, ranging widely in age but being above average in intelligence and increasingly sophisticated in taste. They find our books enjoyable, in part because they have no fear of finding endless profanity or immorality, or page upon page of depression to add to what they read in the newspaper every morning. For that matter, I know of no author of category romance who would write any other way. Like our readers, we are positive people, looking at the brighter side of life, dedicated to problem-solving and, yes, happy endings.

Before the matter of tip sheets and guidelines is set aside, let me say a final word about the "formula" often mentioned by those new to or unfamiliar with the genre. "Formula" has a nasty sound . . . and rightfully so, since it implies that a writer composes a story mechanically. None of us do that! There are no clones in category romance. One doesn't simply sit down and write the same thing over and over again following some elementary set of rules. Each book is written, created, and produced by an author whose emotional investment in the project is monumental. Indeed, with so many books on the market, my colleagues and I spend much of our time laboring to make each plotline, each sentence, paragraph or chapter, unique.

To those cynics who so often ask about the "formula," therefore, my answer is very simple: If there is a "formula" to speak of, it consists ever so broadly of a man, a woman, a love story, and a happy ending. Voilà!

After thoroughly familiarizing yourself with the genre, you will probably want to pick a specific line at which to aim. Based on each publisher's tip sheets, find a line whose specifications most closely resemble your personal preferences. For example, if you want to write a longer novel, something in the range of 70,000 or 75,000 words, set your sights on a Silhouette Special Edition or a Harlequin American Romance. If your proclivity is toward action and adventure, as opposed to inner psychological conflict, think about writing a Silhouette Intimate Moments. If you feel most comfortable with a sensually explicit style, aim for an Ecstasy or one of the other more sensual lines.

With a definite goal in mind, and having read the very latest books published by your target company, you are ready to begin.

Pick a theme that interests you. Since your contemporary romance will be told primarily from the woman's point of view, its theme will most often emanate from her. You may want to write about the conflict between career and family, the problems of love the second time around, the struggle for sexual equality. Whereas in the past, the most common theme was a woman's virginity and her preservation of it, themes have changed drastically, as have the times. Nowadays, with most heroines in their mid-twenties or older, few are virgins, and if they are, they must have extremely good reasons for being so . . . which may indeed be the major theme of the story. Further, the governess-heroine of old has yielded to the female executive, lawyer, photographer, geologist, or architect, hence a corresponding widening of theme possibilities.

Themes today may relate to a woman's attitude toward men based on a past hurt, her attitude toward marriage based on a family trauma, her attitude toward the world based on her own lofty ambitions. You may choose issues of trust, love versus lust, freedom and its many meanings; in short, any of the issues facing a woman of today. Most important, be sure *you* feel comfortable with the major theme, since it is one in which you'll be as emotionally involved as your heroine.

Next, create your characters, giving them names, physical characteristics, occupations and backgrounds, in a sense composing a case study working from present to past. Your characters must be complete, interesting and modern. Research their occupations as though you were entering that field yourself, though you may include a only small fraction of that information in your actual manuscript. Before you ever lift a pencil, you should know your characters intimately. If they are composites of people you've known from time to time, fine. The better you understand them, the easier it will be to write about them. Remember, if *you* aren't drawn to them, your reader won't be!

Above and beyond the conflicts encountered, often created, by the hero and heroine, these two characters must be likable. Indeed, the reader should want to identify with the heroine *and* fall in love with the hero—which does not mean to say that these characters must be perfect. Small faults, when acknowledged by either hero or heroine, often make them all the more endearing.

Conversely, don't hesitate to idealize your characters in some ways. Remember, romance is, in its way, a fantasy. It's all right to make your characters larger than life, as long as they remain, by some stretch of the imagination, believable.

Now, find a situation to introduce your characters to one another. This will be the start of your novel, and is critical to the establishment of both characters and theme. Since category romances are, by definition and guideline, shorter than mainstream novels, there is no time to dally with past relationships that can be handled in summarized flashbacks as the story progresses. Rather, the hero and heroine must meet early on, preferably in Chapter 1, certainly no later than the start of Chapter 2, in circumstances that are enticing—or they will arouse the interest of neither editor nor reader. With the number of new romance novels appearing on the bookstore racks and shelves each month, readers are growing understandably picky. They will give the author ten, perhaps twenty, pages (all skimmed as they stand at the shelves) in which to capture their fancy. If the reader is bored, she will put the book down—and you've lost a sale. Worse, if the editor is bored, your book will never make it to the shelf!

Having chosen an introductory situation that excites you, now sit down and plot out the rest of the story. I prefer to do this with pencil and paper, listing first the general course of events to take place, then gradually filling in detail with each go-round.

At the start of the story, hero and heroine either meet for the very first time, are reunited after a long separation, or are forced, by some twist of fate, to see each other as they've never done before. At story's end, they quite surely declare their love and head toward a future of rainbows and sunshine together. Between those two points . . . the storm rages! Use your imagination; be innovative. Stretch the guidelines as much as possible without breaching them. Look toward everyday life for realism, toward your fantasy life for exhilaration. Be conservatively daring . . . and have fun.

Given the limited number of pages allotted, the story must be tight. I find that I work most comfortably with one major theme and its conflict, and one or two lesser sources of tension, all intertwined to keep the whole flowing quickly and bring about the ultimate confrontation and resolution.

Whereas mainstream fiction can handle many more sub-themes and sub-plots, the category novel is self-limiting. Indeed, the true challenge of writing category fiction—be it romance, mystery, western or science fiction—is in presenting the most meaningful story possible, given the limitations of a mere 200 or 250 pages. And it *is* a challenge. Ask any established writer of another genre who has ever attempted to write in category!

Time can't be wasted with unnecessary detail. Hence, I haven't even *mentioned* the locale of the story. Whereas originally there was a touch of the travelogue in category romance, today the emphasis is on the *relationship*, the love story itself. Indeed, the fact of location has become so inconsequential that I have, on more than one occasion and with remarkable ease, changed it *after* I've begun a book. Obviously, if one plans to write about a hero and heroine meeting and working together as part of an anthropological study on a tiny South Pacific island, things are different. And, in either case, what little or lot you portray of a particular locale should be accurate. With a worldwide readership, there will always be one fan or foe who *knows* whether what you've described is correct.

Just as the setting must be introduced light-handedly, the use of secondary characters must likewise be soft-pedaled. There is simply not enough room to give them depth. Therefore, I usually conceive of these characters last, using them solely to further the storyline, to move the hero and heroine toward one another.

There are times when my plot outline undergoes more editing as I write than the manuscript itself does.

It never fails to thrill me when my characters and story take off by themselves, and I find newer, more exciting things occurring than I had ever planned. In light of this, I reserve the right to toss that original plot outline in the trash if I see fit. Spontaneity, within bounds, can't be beaten!

Plot outline, character descriptions, theme synopses in hand, you are finally ready to begin writing. Choose your words with care, leaning freely toward the sensual, being ever aware that a romance must be abundantly romantic, that you must seduce your reader.

The reader should quickly identify with the heroine and begin to experience life through her eyes. Make it a vibrant life! Let the heroine *do,* rather than constantly ponder, brood, or recall. If she is relaxed and happy, let her warm to the hero, open up in conversation, return his gentle banter. If she is frustrated, let her snap at him waspishly. If she is angry, let her make his scrambled eggs too dry. If she is nervous, let her knot her fingers in a telephone cord or fidget with the fold of a sheet. Such attention to detail makes her all the more real, all the more human.

In keeping with the above, I cannot stress strongly enough the importance of dialogue in today's category romance. It may be intelligent, thought-provoking, poignant, blunt, or humorous. It should be used freely and often, as the most effective vehicle for allowing two people to get to know each other and, indeed, fall in love.

Alas, you are now on your own. For, in the actual word-by-word working of a manuscript, your specific writing style will be as different from mine as night from day. Contrary to popular notion, the field of the category romance welcomes this, just as it welcomes originality and freshness of plot ideas and characters. Herein is the challenge: to work within the guidelines of the category to produce a work that is new and exciting.

Marvelous things have happened in the past few years. Our heroes and heroines have matured and grown more real, more modern. Their situations have broadened to include a whole gamut of circumstances, many in direct turnaround to those of tradition. One thing remains the same, though. Love.

First and foremost, a category romance is a novel about love: finding it, recognizing it, perhaps momentarily losing a grip on it, before finally capturing it forever. To write category romance, one must *feel* romance. One must blend fact with fantasy, emotion with imagination, to produce a story that leaps out to embrace the reader in a fiercely gentle grip. It's not easy, this writing of romance. It takes hour upon hour of intense concentration, week after week of steady work. But for the pride of the finished product, and the pleasure it brings to reader after reader, it is truly a labor of love!

2

ESCAPE TO ROMANCE

by Janet Louise Roberts

Pseudonyms: Louisa Bronte
Rebecca Danton
Janette Radcliffe

Imprints: Ballantine
Dell
Fawcett
Jove
Pocket Books
Warner

A WOMAN comes home from her office or teaching or nursing, or from whatever occupation she makes her living. Her neck hurts from the pressures of the day. She picks up a newspaper, only to find herself dismayed at the bleak events reported.

A housewife finishes the dishes, urges the children to their homework, finds her tired husband asleep in front of the televised ball game.

An older woman, widowed too soon, finds her apartment empty and echoing, with only violence outside on the dark streets.

At times, everyone needs to escape from the stresses and strains of life through books. Romance novels offer readers escape into a glamorous world, into the lives of a lovely young heroine and her handsome hero, who glide through daring adventures in strange and exotic places where readers can forget their troubles for a while.

In addition to the young heroine and her hero, what elements are important to novels of romantic escape? The vital elements are the same in romance novels as in life. Let us consider them.

Setting

The setting for a romance novel is most important. Use your travel experiences, the hotels where you stayed (or have seen advertised or described in brochures or travel and interior decoration sections of newspapers and magazines), houses you saw on guided tours, information in guidebooks, or even city maps to bring the settings to life and make them seem real and appropriate for your heroine. Keep any pictures you have taken on your trips carefully in albums so you can refer to them later as you write your novels; they will help you recall unique details of exotic or strange locales.

As you tour historical restorations, take detailed notes on the furnishings, layout, architecture, and decorations to draw on later as the background for historical or period romances. This gives authenticity and also helps create the right emotional tone and background for your characters' actions.

If it is impossible to travel personally to a place you want to describe, books and magazines, or travel guides, travel films and slides can give exact details that add spice to your descriptions. Browse in the library, look for books that go into specific detail about just how the place looks, and feels, and smells.

Look around you. Wherever you are is someone else's paradise. You are in a unique place right this minute.

Describe it so someone in a desert can visualize the rivers, the plantation homes, the azaleas you picture for them.

Shelter

Heroine and hero may stroll barefoot at dawn along a beach, holding hands, returning to a grass-covered hut for their breakfast of sweet rolls, fresh pineapple, and steaming coffee.

She sits demurely opposite her scowling employer at luncheon. The glass-topped table is set on the patio of his exquisite island home. Purple bougainvillea rambles up the sides of the gazebo beside them. Beyond, the oval swimming pool shimmers azure in the sunlight.

Does your heroine live in an "ordinary" small town in a farm state? A reader in a noisy city will appreciate reading about your heroine's quiet country lanes, the golden wheat fields, fishing in a lazy stream, as she daydreams about her hero. Perhaps your heroine lives in a house facing a mountain. Tell the reader what it is like to climb a mountain, to see a rainbow at sunset. Let your heroine sit on a rock and gaze out over a green valley.

Appeal to all the senses—describe the colors, flower scents, foods, perfumes, the bitter and the sweet. It is not trite to describe a sunset in Alaska, or a rainbow in Hawaii, a mountaintop in the Rockies, or a cactus flower in the desert. The reader cannot actually be there, but she wants you to take her there as she reads. Don't disappoint her! After she has followed you all the way to the garden, show and tell her about the flowers. Describe, describe!

Music wafts from the brightly lighted resort hotel. She listens, leaning against a folded beach umbrella, and feels as if her heart is breaking. He flew back to the

States this morning, without a word or a note to her! A cool breeze chills her heated body, and the scent of frangipani from her leis is overpowering.

It is not just the love story that your reader wants to entertain and satisfy her. Part of the romance is found in the beauty of the surroundings.

Food

In a romance novel, food can add much glamour. For example, in writing a book set in the Caribbean, I always bring in the exotic dishes, made of rice, black beans, mangoes, passion fruit, coconut, pineapple. If a writer is unable to travel to exotic places—to the Bahamas, St. Croix, Puerto Rico, or to Hawaii, Japan, Indonesia—the solution is as close as the nearest library. The cookbook section overflows with books on international and regional cooking. The hero will take the heroine to a dimly lighted restaurant on the beach and ply her with Mai Tais, while the ocean waves roll against the white sands, and the silver moon hangs in the night-blue sky.

Describe the colors, the flavors, the textures of the native foods, but don't stop the action and dialogue while the heroine plows through a seven-course meal. Interweave the descriptions with the ongoing actions and conversation of your characters.

Descriptions of foods indigenous to a particular region or foreign country help create the appropriate atmosphere and mood, and give the feeling of authenticity to a romance novel. As she reads about exotic foods and strange drinks, what fruits grow in the area, what kinds of fish the local fishermen are bringing in, the reader comes to feel part of the new setting and background you are describing.

For example:

The brilliant sun promised a hot day. Jenny came down to breakfast, fresh in her white shorts and blue striped shirt, and sat down at the glass table in the patio. Maria gave her a broad grin as she placed the dish of golden papaya before her.

Jenny squeezed lime on it, then spooned the first delicious mouthful. She gazed thoughtfully at the sparkling blue sea beyond the sandy beach. If Ted was in a filthy mood again today, she would escape to the boat, and sail all morning.

She poured out steaming black coffee, added lumps of brown sugar, lavishly, and munched on a crisp croissant. Maybe she would ask Sue to go with her. The child adored sailing, and it would keep both of them out of her uncle's stormy path.

The more you can draw your reader into the different, glamorous world you have created and make her see and feel and experience the excitement and emotion of your heroine (by appealing to her sense of smell, touch, sight, sound, and taste), the more she will enjoy your story.

Clothing

Details of clothes can add much to the reader's pleasure in a novel. Most women enjoy pretty clothes. Historical novels abound in opportunities to describe Empire dresses, a Victorian hoop skirt, ruffles, frills and unusual colors. Consult period fashion books to help you choose the correct details for a special time in history.

For contemporary romances, buy the latest fashion magazines, American and European. Let luscious silks, wools, linens, in the most daring or feminine styles adorn your heroines.

Clothes can be used effectively by romance writers in

several other ways. Just as a young woman in real life will wear one outfit to go sailing on a yacht in the Caribbean, and quite a different one in a San Francisco disco, so should your heroine wear different clothes for different occasions, settings, and periods.

Clothing styles and colors not only enable the readers to visualize the scene, but also give it a romantic touch. When the heroine wears a silky silver-blue negligee that half reveals her seductive nightdress—the reader knows sensual excitement is in store. Study fashion magazines, read ad copy! And dream up your own styles for your heroine. All of this is part of creating the romantic picture.

But don't make it a style show—unless a style show is part of your plot! Interweave descriptions of the clothing with the action. Show the heroine getting dressed as she worries about the evening ahead. Describe the gown as she turns sideways to get the hoops through the narrow door leading to the back garden. Perhaps the creamy lace sleeve rips as the hero grabs her arms to shake—or embrace—her. Lights, camera, action!

The hero should wear clothing typical of the local setting, and if the story takes place in Hawaii, his Hawaiian shirt will set off his "teak tan." Or he may be sternly handsome in his black tuxedo and white ruffled shirt.

The heroine, however, should have most of the reader's attention. A small blonde with green eyes will be fetching in a flowered cotton dress with ruffles circling her tanned arms.

If the scene of your contemporary romance is a New York night club, your tall brunette heroine will attract attention as she glides in wearing a scarlet silk harem-pants suit, and the diamond collar given to her by the forceful, devilish man with her will be prominently displayed.

When I write character dossiers—which I do for every person in every novel—I include favorite colors with each one as part of her personality. I believe a person's favorite colors tell much about him or her. After I decide what color hair and eyes a character has, and how tall she is, then I select her color schemes. This helps immensely to bring the character to life for the reader.

These are the basic elements of the romance novel. Why does anyone go on a vacation? To see something different, to eat different foods, wear different clothing, to meet a dashing hero (at least in her imagination) and have a romantic adventure. The reader of a romance novel hopes to find in it an escape from the mundane, everyday routines, monotony, the dreary and sometimes what seems the overwhelming events of her life. Everyone needs fantasy, and women who read romances—as they are doing by the millions today—need to act out in fantasy what cannot be realized in their daily lives. Events may be beyond their control, but in reading the romance novel, they can be assured of a happy ending.

I like to imagine heroines who are good young women whom I can admire. I like heroes who try hard to do the right thing, who will struggle and fight for others and for causes in which they believe. I like both to be generous givers of themselves, rather than selfish takers.

Are romantic novels unrealistic? Or are they, rather, an ideal, hoped for, but rarely attained?

3

CHARACTERIZATION IN THE ROMANCE NOVEL

by Laurie McBain

Imprint: Avon Books

"I COULDN'T put the book down, and I was up till three o'clock in the morning reading it. I just had to find out how the story ended. I was wondering, if you wouldn't mind, could you tell me what happened to the characters later on? I was curious to know if. . . ."

Those are probably the most gratifying words an author can hear. I wonder if there was ever anyone who has read *Gone With The Wind* who, after turning that last page and reading those final, unforgettable words of Rhett Butler's, did not sit for a moment and speculate about what might happen later in the lives of those two immortal characters that Margaret Mitchell had created from her imagination? Did Scarlett manage to recapture Rhett's affections? Did they ever meet again? Did Rhett remain deaf to her protestations of love? Could he forget her? Or did he find someone else to love? And those are just a few of the many possibilities.

But why all of that interest? Why do people care? Why do the readers want to know something more about these people who existed only between the pages of a book? When the book was made into a movie, why did it become of national concern that just the right actor and actress portray those characters on the screen? Because the characters Margaret Mitchell created in *Gone With The Wind* captured the imagination of its readers.

Along with these characters, readers experience the turbulence of life during the Civil War. Through the eyes of these characters, readers know all the pains and joys of living, as if they were there, riding in that wagon along that dusty road of red Georgia clay, as Scarlett escapes from the horrors of the burning of Atlanta. And when Scarlett arrives at Tara, where she finds her strength and purpose to survive, readers feel both relief and sadness, for although she is safe, Tara and the life Scarlett had known there are gone forever.

To create a memorable story with characters that will engage the emotions of the reader, is the ultimate goal of the storyteller. But how do you as a writer achieve this goal? How do you bring those people of your imagination to life? How do you give them a past? A future? How do you get inside of their minds? And, most important, how do you share this knowledge with the reader? How do you get the reader to care?

First, you must create a character, and you must believe in this character if you expect the reader to.

But how? I continue to feel a sense of amazement with the creation of each character, for whether hero, heroine, or secondary characters, their birth and growth can be a mystifying experience for the writer. Once you have brought this character to life, you must be prepared to have him or her begin living *his* or *her* life, which might mean that this individual has a different idea from yours about what he or she intends to do in your novel. As soon as these characters begin to grow, they will touch the lives of all of your characters, perhaps in a way you originally may not have intended.

When I was writing *Dark Before the Rising Sun*—an historical novel set in 18th-century England, which concerned a man's return home after an absence of over fifteen years—I had to come up with a name for the child of the hero and heroine. I thought of different names, discarded them, then, finally, settled on one I thought would be appropriate—but it was not just any name. I named the child Christopher. Why? And why make it special? Surely, any name would have sufficed? I named the child Christopher because of another character in the novel, and because of that decision, Captain Sedgewick Christopher, who until then had been just a vague figure from the past who had helped the hero, suddenly became a significant character. He had not been a character I was going to develop, especially since he had already been long dead and buried when the story began. He was just a shadowy figure, to be mentioned in passing, until now, when I forged a link between characters. Suddenly Sedgewick Christopher became more than just a name, and the link between these characters gave reason for the subsequent actions of the hero.

Through the words of a dead man, in a letter read by the hero, this character came back to life. He became a flesh-and-blood man, with a poignant tale to tell. The letter also served to explain much about the hero's past life and how this man had influenced him. So now, not only does the reader have a keener insight into the hero's past, but the reader has learned of another man's life, how that man's actions affected the lives of the hero and heroine and influenced the naming of their son! The hero, having come to look upon this man as he would have his own father, honored him by naming his first-born son after him. Although the reader never truly meets this Captain Sedgewick Christopher, my aim was to make sure the reader would be touched by his life.

Now you have a reason for what happened, and your characters are no longer just cardboard cut-outs, but people with feelings. Thus when readers think of Alastair Marlowe, a young man the hero rescued (in much the same manner in which Sedgewick Christopher had rescued him years before), they will understand the hero's motivations. At first it might have appeared that there were four diverse characters: a child to be named; a dour old sea captain; a young gentleman who had been given a second chance; and the hero, a man who'd had to fight to regain his self-respect. But now, because three of these characters were provided with a past, and their lives crossed fatefully, the fourth one, the child, has a future linked directly to those past chance encounters. The linkage in the chain of events that began with the name of a seemingly insignificant character is now complete.

Rhea Claire Leighton, the heroine of *Dark Before the Rising Sun*, became a living person to me when I realized that despite the separation I had planned between her and the hero, I could not follow that original plan. I had portrayed Rhea Claire, throughout the novel, as a gentle, understanding woman, and as I approached the denouement, I suddenly knew that all of my careful plotting would have to go for naught, because, if I were to be true to this character, if I were not to betray her, then I could not have her abandon the hero when he needed her the most.

I think this must be the point at which you either succeed or fail in bringing your characters to life. You put aside your cleverness and plot twists and, above all else, think of the credibility of your main character. In another novel I might have written, the heroine probably would have left the hero, thus prolonging the anxieties of the reader, but not Rhea Claire, not this particular heroine. If I expected to have the reader believe in this heroine, then I could not have her act out of character toward the end of the book just to heighten the suspense.

On the other hand, there can be difficulties when you come to look upon your characters as real people. In *Tears of Gold,* a novel I set in Gold Rush California, I had a character that became too real, and too dear to me. It hadn't started out that way, but being a bit of a rogue, and quite charming, he found his way into my heart, even though I knew that he was going to have to come to an unfortunate end. In this case, if I hadn't followed my original storyline and allowed Brendan O'Flynn, the heroine's brother, to live, it would have been detrimental to the story. For this Irish fortune hunter not to have met his end when he did would have changed the story completely. Because of the type of man Brendan O'Flynn was, the reader was expecting the worst to happen, and just because I took a liking to him, I couldn't allow my personal feelings to change what the plot line demanded. Brendan O'Flynn would have met his end tragically sooner or later, and because I had created Brendan O'Flynn in a certain manner, I now had to stand back and allow his fate to catch up to him, despite my wishes to do otherwise.

Do not be afraid to make your characters different. A many-faceted character, like an intricately-cut, highly-polished gem, shines the brightest and catches the eye.

In *Chance the Winds of Fortune,* the hero was a privateer whom the reader might not have expected to display an exceptional amount of charity towards his fellow man—or beast—but aboard his ship was a cat named Jamaica. The captain had rescued the stray cat from drowning, and from that day forward the cat had been a highly respected member of the crew. Also on board the *Sea Dragon* was a young orphan, whom the captain had rescued from a brutal existence. These two unfortunate characters allowed me to show a side of the hero that few people had ever seen. It was an important facet that needed to be examined, for it was a personality trait that helped to shape the hero's character in relationship to other characters in the novel. It also served as a balance against the sometimes cold arrogance of the man, and made him more likable.

Lady Kate, the villain of that same novel, had all of the anxieties and fears of normal people, but murderous intentions as well. She also had a rather perverse sense of humor. Some of the more humorous—as well as some of the more terrifying—situations occurred with this character. Perhaps that is why those situations became all the more startling and horrifying, because for one moment the reader was smiling with this character, even while knowing she was up to no good.

Lady Kate was a tragic figure. Dressed in black and wearing a single red rose, her face masked, she plotted her revenge, all the while humming nostalgic songs, and in the end, causing tragedy and death. By showing some of the more humorous, as well as bizarre, quirks of her personality, along with her difficulties in hiring any competent henchmen to help her carry out her revenge, readers were caught up in her life as they wouldn't have been had she remained some vague, threatening, shadowy figure. She had been driven into madness by her life of misadventure, and, in the end, was herself a victim of it. But, by having delved deeper into this woman's mind through showing her in confrontations with others, and by traveling with her on her journey toward her ultimate destruction, I tried to make the reader feel the hate and madness that drove her to her death, and perhaps to feel a moment's pity for her.

The key to remember is that each and every character in a novel is motivated by something or someone. Each and every character will react, in a different way, whether passively or aggressively. And each reaction will have an effect on the story and on the other characters, for they are all interwoven. As a writer, you are creating a tapestry with countless threads of varying shades and colors, which, when woven together, become a smooth, seamless fabric, with a story unfolding in images made up of subtle shapes and sharp angles, all blending together to create the dramatic scene depicted.

Trying to create characters that are believable is often a process of trial and error, of shaping and re-shaping of characters: of the deletion of some, and the addition of others. But, in the end, readers will have come to know what these characters are thinking and feeling, and will have experienced life through these characters' eyes. Perhaps, when they have finished the novel, readers will still wonder about these characters and what might be happening in their lives tomorrow, or even a year from now.

4

SELLING THE REGENCY ROMANCE TODAY

by Donna Meyer

Pseudonym: Megan Daniel

Imprint: New American Library/Signet

I WRITE romances. More specifically, I write Regency romances. I've been writing them for three years.

Before writing my first book, *Amelia,* I'd never written a word for publication. Yet that first book was bought, unagented, by the first publisher I submitted it to.

Sound easy? Don't be fooled. Like all writing, a successful Regency requires hard work. Fewer Regencies are being published today than a few years ago. But their fans are loyal, and the market is steady.

It may be harder to break in now than when I began, but if you do your homework and can write well, the market will open wide to you.

What is a Regency romance? Most simply, it's a short romantic novel set in England during the period from roughly 1800 to 1825, and deals almost exclusively with the small world of the English upper class with its particular code of honor and morality, its insular view of the world, and its devotion to order, manners, and fashion. It was a time when class lines were rigid, consumption by the wealthy was conspicious, and marriages were often arranged to promote family ties. High-stakes gambling, luxurious carriages, beautiful clothes, fox hunts, wit, and perfect manners were the stuff of daily life.

When you type the words "A Regency Romance" below your title, you enter into a contract with your reader, a promise to follow the rules those words imply. When she honors her part of the contract by paying for your book, she has the right to get what she's been promised.

If you're considering writing a Regency, you've probably read several. But you may not have read them analytically. Now you must. It's the old maxim, "Study the market."

Before beginning *Amelia,* I read over a hundred Regencies from the classics of Jane Austen to the delightful tales of Georgette Heyer, Clare D'Arcy, and Joan Smith. Obviously, to read so many of them, one had better enjoy them. I do. For any writer, however talented, to try writing the kind of book she doesn't enjoy and respect is cruel and unusual punishment—and useless besides.

Let's take a closer look at how to write a Regency with a good chance of selling.

As I read all those Regencies, I had a pen in my hand, underlining everything that gave each book its distinctive sound and made it a Regency Romance rather than simply a story set in Regency England.

Examples? Imagine you're analyzing my Regency,

The Unlikely Rivals. You'd underline period details like, "The chaise bumped across the cobbles and drew to a stop. The steps were let down for Saskia to alight." Or, "She had to see to the hiring of an intimidating butler, two footmen, a housemaid-nanny for the twins, a pair of kitchenmaids for Mrs. Jansen, plus the abigail Aunt Hester insisted was *de rigueur*." You'd note descriptions of elaborate meals with dishes such as roast leveret, cockscombs in red wine, and haricot of vegetables. Distinctive dialogue would be underlined, such as, "Naturally I should not wish to be thought unmindful of my filial duty," or "Really, what a perfectly cork-brained notion." And you'd pay attention to Mrs. van Houten's day dress of amethyst levantine topped with a spencer of dove-grey silk.

None of these telling details would be found in a Harlequin or Silhouette. And that, of course, is just the point.

All the underlined information went onto 3×5 cards and was filed under headings like Fashion, Slang, Food and Drink, Carriages, etc. Soon I began to get a vivid picture of what is important in a Regency (clothes, formal speech, descriptions of meals, facial expression) and what is not (politics, religion, the cost of things, work). More important, the distinctive "voice" of a Regency, the sense of language and pace, became almost second nature to me.

Next came the crucial step of historic research. I read histories, biographies, and diaries, studied costume books and old cookbooks, looked at paintings, and pored over maps and guidebooks. Don't stint on this step. Regency fans are faithful and know a great deal about Regency England. If you put Windsor Castle in

London instead of Windsor, they'll know you haven't done your homework, and you'll lose them. You must know even more than they do.

My most helpful sources were period newspapers and magazines. They're filled with minutiae that bring the period alive: the cost of a horse, the description of an estate to let, want ads for lady's maids, and social gossip. There are serialized love stories, patterns for making lace, and household hints. Nothing could put you more firmly into the mind of a Regency lady.

Another indispensable tool is an 1816 map of London I found in the library and had copied. I refer to it constantly to decide where my characters live, check routes and distances, or put buildings and parks in context. Often just looking at that map can spur my sluggish mind into new directions.

Research can be fun and enlightening, but eventually a writer has to write. She has to begin covering blank pages with words.

I always begin with plot. Or rather, the germ of a plot. Often it's a very small germ indeed which may well disappear entirely before my plot is complete. But it gets me started.

Consider the germ that began my book, *The Unlikely Rivals*. It was an offhand comment from my husband: "Send them on a scavenger hunt." An intriguing notion.

With one tiny idea like that in mind, I sit down with my writer-husband, a large pot of coffee, and a yellow legal pad to play "What if. . .?" This is a free-wheeling brainstorming session in which anything goes. *Do not* become an editor at this point. No idea is too outlandish to consider. For example: What if the whole future rests on the scavenger hunt? What if the hero thinks the heroine is a man? What if she challenges him to a duel

to get him out of the competition? What are they looking for? What if they both win? Or neither does? What if
he's a great horseman and she sneezes whenever she
gets near one? And so on.

Ninety-nine percent of those ideas were eventually
thrown out, but with the other one percent I finally
came up with a usable plot.

Only one element is absolutely essential to a Regency
plot: The Romance. Whatever else occurs, the hero and
heroine, their attraction, their misunderstandings and
problems, and the final resolution of their love, must be
central to the story. There can and should be interesting
and funny sub-plots, but you mustn't stray too far from
the central romance.

By the same reasoning, only two characters are essential: the hero and heroine. They must be attractive and
appealing, though they should have enough physical or
mental quirks to make them human and interesting.
She must be bright, well-educated, genteel, and fairly
independent, someone the reader can both identify
with and idealize. He must be handsome, though not in
a cardboard, comic-book hero way, masculine, and
strong, with enough faults and vulnerabilities to make
him endearing. He should be wealthy or have a chance
to become so. A Regency heroine does not live her hap-
pily-ever-after in genteel poverty though she might start
out that way. His job is to take her away from all that.

Formerly, Regency heroines were usually young and
definitely virginal. A recent trend, indicative of the romance market as a whole, is toward older, wiser, and
more experienced heroines. There is still more restraint
than in the explicit contemporary romances—
remember the strict moral code of the period—but
there is more erotic tension in Regencies today. The

heroine might be a widow, or she might allow the hero more than a chaste kiss on the last page. In at least one notable example, she actually makes love to him, but it's clear they will soon sanctify the bond with holy wedlock.

The other characters can be as varied as your imagination can make them. Have fun with them. I have successfully used fops and dandies, servants and neighbors, old people full of advice for or outrage against the young, law officers, children, and of course villains.

One of the most effective ways to draw character is with dialogue. Regency dialogue is clearly different from that of a contemporary romance. Modern Americans tend to be sloppy talkers using verbal short-cuts and slang. The English upper crust of the early nineteenth century chose their words with precision and a sense of formality. Look at these examples from my own work and compare them to how the same idea might be expressed today.

"I should be much obliged if you would keep your rather overblown opinions to yourself, sir." vs. "Oh, shut up!" "It is true that he is perhaps a trifle thinner than is commonly thought attractive." vs. "He's skinny as a rail."

Of course, slang is common in all periods and judiciously used, period slang such as "needle-witted" for smart or "forty-jawed" for talkative can lend a nice sense of period and character. But be careful. Young Ladies of Quality did *not* use slang, and even a sporting gentleman puffing a cheroot and drinking Blue Ruin with his friends can quickly become incomprehensible. That might be your goal as in this passage from my book, *The Reluctant Suitor,* when Geoff says,

> "Of all the bacon-brained, paper-skulled, muttonheaded starts, this takes the cake! Tell you what it is, Mama. You're

dicked in the nob. Got some maggot or other in your head. To try to fob such a Canterbury tale off on the *ton*! It's the Bank of England to a Charley's shelter that all the world and his wife'll twig it quick as the cat can lick her ear. Then we *will* be in the basket!"

The reader needn't actually understand what he's saying, only that he's upset, but you can see how easily period slang can become nearly indecipherable.

I always read my dialogue aloud or, better yet, have someone read it to me. This makes it easy to spot inconsistencies and unnaturalness. You can hear if something doesn't fit the character or have the distinctive voice of a Regency.

Now you must put all these intriguing characters and their antic doings in the proper setting. Their world must be luxurious, elegant, well-ordered, and beautifully described, a place so different from twentieth century America that the reader knows from the first page that she has entered another world.

Because Regencies are not terribly sensual they must be very *sensuous*, lush with sounds and smells and the details of period and place. In *The Sensible Courtship*, I introduce Francesca, the heroine, in her bath.

> A nondescript little tune escaped the young woman's lips as she soaked in the warm, scented bath, a counter-point to the tinkle of water as it dribbled from her fingertips. The soap, the finest available, smelled of violets from Devonshire and made a rich, creamy lather as she eased it over her white skin, drawing large, lazy circles across her shoulders and breasts.
>
> A busy little maid, a pert smile belying her air of industry, stirred up the coals, poured more steaming water into the tub, and began to scrub her mistress's back.

Setting is so important that after I've finished my first

draft, I go through it with an eye to making the setting more vivid. By adding details like the swoosh of a silken gown, the glare of a highly polished ballroom floor, or the pungent smell of a just-snuffed candle, I make it easier for my reader to leave today behind and enter the world I've created.

You're finished. Congratulations! But before sending off your manuscript, go through it again. Check for historical inaccuracies. Have you referred to Waterloo a year before it happened? Have you had a real person speaking five years after he died?

Read your dialogue aloud again. Could it be brightened with some period slang or a more formal construction? Perhaps a touch of dialect? Can lively dialogue be substituted anywhere for dull narrative?

Check also for anachronisms. Have you referred to a drunken gentleman as "smashed" or "drunk as a skunk" instead of "bosky" or "in his altitudes"? Does your hero wear pants instead of pantaloons or a tie instead of a cravat? Do the characters' thoughts and actions arise from the assumptions of today rather than from those of the Regency? Take time to fix any such errors.

All is well. You're finished. Send it off, take a vacation, relax. Until, that is, the next hero and heroine begin chattering in your mind, refusing to be silenced. Eventually, you'll have to let them out. Eventually, you'll have to type once more those ominous words, *Chapter One.*

5

THE CONTEMPORARY LIGHT ROMANCE

by Margaret Major Cleaves and
Sondra Stanford

MARGARET MAJOR CLEAVES
Pseudonym: Ann Major
Imprints: Dell Candlelight Romance
Silhouette Romances

SONDRA STANFORD
Imprints: Harlequin Books
Silhouette Romances

LIKE the flash of a fairy godmother's magic wand, the flip of the first page of a light romance novel can transport a woman of any age into a world of passion and desire, where she is young and beautiful, gowned in swirling silk, whisked to exotic locales, courted by a man who is tall, dark and singularly attractive, and given the happy ending of her dream. The glass slipper always fits the slender foot of the modern-day Cinderella.

Sound appealing? Millions of readers think so, and as a result, the contemporary light romance is a vast and rapidly expanding market, wide open to the new writer.

If you're a beginning writer struggling with the complexities of trying to write a long novel, the modern light romance market might be for you. Since the story is contemporary, much less research is involved than in an historical novel. A light romance is actually a "piece"

35

of a longer book—the love story lifted out. Thus, mastering this genre could be the first step to a larger, more ambitious novel.

Light romances are usually around 50,000–60,000 words in length—another plus for the beginner. One can write three or four books in the length of time it would take to write a single longer novel. This means three or four submissions to editors instead of one and the possibilities of a sale are greatly increased. Because of their brevity, light romances are much less complicated to revise than a longer work. This is an excellent place for aspiring novelists to begin and to earn money from their writing.

These novels are written in the third person and for the most part from the heroine's viewpoint. Occasionally, the hero's viewpoint might also be shown. The heroine is generally between the ages of eighteen and thirty-six, lovely (though perhaps unaware of it), and usually a working girl. She has high principles and ideals. Although she may have dreams of a "Mr. Right" entering her life someday, she is not actively seeking him, and when the hero comes into the picture, she does not immediately realize he is that man. She may even, in fact, believe herself in love with another man.

The hero is usually between thirty and forty years old, handsome in a rough-hewn fashion, well established in business or a profession, often wealthy. He is a commanding figure, self-confident, capable, even arrogant, yet he avoids pomposity by having a sense of humor. Regrettably, some authors equate violence with love, and occasionally show the hero being physically abusive to the heroine (one can only suppose this is to demonstrate his male superiority), but by and large, this kind of behavior is frowned upon by editors and by readers, too.

The moment the hero enters the novel, the heroine is at once strongly attracted to him—against her will—although she usually denies this vehemently both to herself and to him through the first chapters of the book. The following excerpt from Ann Major's *Wild Lady* illustrates the hero's immediate and forceful impact upon the heroine:

> He towered over her—all arrogant six feet four inches of him. There were lines at the corners of his lips and beneath his cobalt blue eyes and between his dark brows that hadn't been there five years ago. His skin was bronzed, his auburn hair streaked gold from the sun. He was as handsome as always—even more handsome than she remembered.
>
> Just looking at him—and she was aching all over.

Both central characters should be painstakingly described. Careful attention should be given the heroine's clothes.

From the first moment the hero and heroine meet there should be conflict. In her novel, *Golden Tide*, Sondra Stanford handled the initial conflict between the two lovers as follows:

> "You've got the power to either send your brother to prison or to keep him free."
>
> A chill climbed Melody's spine and her hands felt suddenly icy. She licked her dry lips and asked with foreboding, "Wh-what do I have to do?"
>
> "You have to marry me again," he said in a voice of steel.

As the story progresses and the heroine is aware of her growing attraction for the hero, the conflict intensifies, building to a crisis—with only occasional respites of tenderness, quickly followed by new misunderstandings. The crisis usually occurs in the next-to-the-last chapter but is happily resolved in the last chapter.

While the light romance novel avoids explicit sex,

it relies heavily on sensuous descriptions. Increasingly, the trend in romantic fiction is toward more realistic and sensual stories. Words that appeal to the senses— taste, touch, and smell—are vital. The emotional tone is all-important, and the love scenes must convey a high level of intense feeling. Note the conspicuous romance detail in this passage from Sondra Stanford's *Bellefleur:*

> She tried to pull away from him, but his hold was too strong. She was forced to mumble into his collar. "Bill, I . . . I . . ." She could get no further. He was nibbling . . . definitely nibbling . . . at her earlobe, and that and his soft breath that was tickling her neck was driving her crazy with desire. Her limbs suddenly felt about as sturdy as jelly and she grew panic-stricken. "Let me go!" she exclaimed breathlessly.

While other characters—often *the other woman*—are important to round out a story or to provide complications, they must never be as well drawn as the two main characters. Describe them briefly, utilize them where necessary, but never, never allow them or their problems to overshadow those of the heroine.

The setting should always be contemporary. The places can be faraway and exotic—Venice, the Riviera, the Caribbean. Or it can be in the United States. Small Town, U.S.A. can be exotic and exciting so long as it is viewed with a fine eye for color and flair. Whatever the setting, the author should romanticize it so that it intensifies the love story rather than detracts from it. Images of gondolas floating dreamily down a Venetian canal or whisps of an Italian serenade should be included rather than a description of how filthy the canal is.

Certain subjects should be scrupulously avoided in these light romances: drugs, alcoholism, sexual perversions, gambling addiction, murder, and violence. Divorce, if included, should be handled very carefully.

"And they lived happily ever after . . ." The last few pages of the book are vitally important. In the last chapter—and not until—the lovers should discover what the reader has known all along: that they are destined for one another. Misunderstandings should be cleared up, and conflicts resolved. A brief paragraph or two to wrap things up is not sufficient. The reader wants a thrilling, uplifting, happy ending, and the author had better not cheat her out of it, no matter how weary she is or how anxious to mail the manuscript. The reader has paid good, hard-earned money for a romantic novel, and she deserves to have the most satisfactory ending a writer can devise.

Frequently, these novels end with the lovers locked in a tight embrace declaring their everlasting love, as in this excerpt from Major's *Touch of Fire:*

"I wish . . . I could convince you I love you and only you," he muttered hoarsely.

She ran her fingers through his thick, tumbling hair and drew his head down so that his sensual mouth hovered above hers. "I think you're smart enough to find a way," she said, arching her body against him.

His lips quirked before curving into a knowing grin. "Why . . . you impudent little tease," he groaned, pulling her closer.

"I'm not . . . teasing," she returned huskily, mesmerized by his intense gaze.

"You damn sure better not be," he whispered before his lips lowered to hers, lingering, tantalizing, sending molten waves of desire pulsing through her arteries as though his very touch were fire.

Satin rustled as he pressed her backward upon the bed, and the sheer intensity of his passion silenced her doubts about his love forever.

Writing for a series line has certain restrictions that general novels do not have; for any writer who aspires to join the ranks, it is a MUST to study the market. This requirement cannot be emphasized strongly enough. Read at least thirty of these books before you even attempt to write one. Notice how many chapters constitute a book, how many words a chapter. Notice the language. Romance has its own voice. Such words as "ruthless, relentless, sardonic, mocking, cynical," and many others are favorites of this genre. For each book that you read, write a couple of sentences describing the action of each chapter. You should be able to outline an entire book on a single sheet of paper. When you have thirty outlines in your hand, the structure of these novels should be clear. Even though this sounds like a lot of extra work, it is necessary. You cannot write for a market until you know the market. Each publisher has his own particular requirements, and it is also advisable to write for writer guidelines.

When you have done your homework, it is time to get started. You may be wondering how much to write before you submit your first novel. The answer varies from editor to editor. Some editors prefer complete novels from unpublished authors, while others prefer partial manuscripts for a light romance, i.e., the first three chapters plus a ten- to twenty-page outline of the remaining chapters. This outline should be written in paragraph form in the present tense. The story should flow smoothly and be interesting—as though the editor were actually reading a condensed version of your novel. Occasionally (but not necessarily) you might even include a snatch of dialogue here and there. Add a brief letter telling the editor of any credits you have.

While most editors cannot offer a contract to an unknown writer from such a synopsis, they can readily tell from reading it whether they would be interested in seeing the completed manuscript. If so, they might send you a letter suggesting revisions. It is easier to change an outline than a book that has already been completely written.

How long should you wait for a response on your manuscript? Again, it varies from publisher to publisher, but a safe bet is eight to ten weeks. If you haven't heard by then, a polite note of reminder is not out of order.

The question of payment is always a fascinating one to a writer, but contract agreements are very individualized. A first-time author naturally cannot command the same advance as an established writer, with numerous books to her credit, but the payment, even for a beginner, is respectable.

In today's booming contemporary romance market, the writer who is willing to work hard and follow a required format can soon be writing a "happily ever after" story in real life. And making a pleasant fairy tale come true isn't half bad!

6

"HAD-I-BUT-KNOWN": HOW TO USE IT IN PLOTTING ROMANTIC SUSPENSE

by Barbara Mertz

Pseudonyms: Barbara Michaels
Elizabeth Peters

Imprints: Dodd, Mead
Congdon & Weed

PART 1

THAT diabolically irreverent versifier, Ogden Nash, is responsible for popularizing the phrase "Had I But Known" (HIBK for short) as a description of one school of detective fiction. Romantic suspense fiction is supposed to be particularly prone to this weakness, and, admittedly, Gothic heroines often intone sentences beginning, "If I had but known what horrors lurked in the ancient hall of Castle Grimly. . . ." But romantic suspense is not the only genre to display HIBK characteristics, and some of the tricks mentioned by Nash are indispensable to all forms of suspense fiction.

The naïve narrator who hears a stealthy creak in the tower where the body lies, and nonchalantly proceeds to investigate it, is the subject of one of Nash's funniest verses. Humor aside, this is the most basic plot problem of the romantic suspense novel. Without danger to the heroine, there is no suspense, and no story. If the heroine is a professional—police officer, spy, or private eye—the author need not explain why she decides to investigate. It is part of her job. But my heroines are mostly amateurs—people like you and me. This increases the strength of reader identification, but makes it difficult to construct a situation in which the girl is imperilled by forces she cannot control or escape. Let's invent a plot.

Our heroine, Jane Jones, is a young girl of good family, beautiful, impoverished and upright, who accepts a position as governess in a remote part of England. After arriving at Castle Grimly, she experiences a series of terrifying events, culminating in an attempt on her life. Why doesn't she pack her portmanteau and leave?

Somewhat to my surprise (for my mind is not usually so orderly), the answers to this vital question fell neatly into outline form.

A. *She doesn't want to leave.*

1. She has fallen madly in love with the hero and cannot bear to leave him.

This is one of the commonest motives used in Gothic novels. It is also one of the weakest and least convincing. The *reader* is not madly in love with the hero, who is often moody, broody, scarred, and otherwise uncomfortable to be around. Modern readers lack patience with a girl so irrationally infatuated.

2. She loves, or feels a sense of responsibility for, another character, usually the child she has been hired to teach.

The only objection I have to this device is that it has been used so often. It can be used effectively, if the personalities of the heroine and the potential victim are properly developed. Mary Stewart did it splendidly in *Nine Coaches Waiting* by portraying a wistful, engaging child and a spunky, conscientious heroine. However, the danger to the child (aged grandmother, simple-minded youth) should arise legitimately from the exigencies of the plot, and not be attributable to a wandering homicidal maniac or kidnapper.

3. She has not accomplished the purpose for which she came to Castle Grimly.

In this case her purpose must be strong, if she is willing to risk life and limb to achieve it. Clearing her unjustly imprisoned brother, discovering the fate of the sister who vanished at Grimly five years earlier, searching for her roots or her missing lover—such motives as these might impel a woman to investigate a funny noise in the tower, or do anything else necessary—but the motive must be established, or at least hinted at, before the action begins.

4. Her own survival or sanity depends on solving the mystery of Castle Grimly.

This is another commonly used trick, and its effectiveness varies (as what does not?) with the skill of the writer. I tried to use this, combined with point #2 above, in a contemporary ghost story, *Ammie Come Home*. The person threatened was the niece of my middle-aged heroine, whom she loved like a daughter; and since the threat was supernatural, its early manifestations were vague enough to be written off as bad dreams or hallucinations. By the time the heroine realized that her niece was possessed by the spirit of a former occupant of Castle Grimly (a house in Georgetown, in this case), the damage had been done; the threat would follow wherever they went, and the only hope of escape was to find the cause of the haunting.

5. She doesn't realize until too late that she is threatened.

As has been noted, this was another of the ploys I

used in *Ammie Come Home*. There are difficulties in the method. If the threat is so vague that the heroine doesn't sense it, the reader may not notice it either. Conversely, if, by clues and plants, the reader is made aware of approaching peril as he ought to be, the heroine would be pretty stupid to miss those hints. I find dreams and similar portents extremely useful in this context; they can be intensely horrifying, but not actively threatening.

6. For reasons of egotism and/or consummate curiosity, the heroine appoints herself amateur detective.

This is probably the weakest excuse of all, though I have used it many times myself. One of my favorite heroines, Amelia Peabody, in *Crocodile on the Sandbank* and *The Curse of the Pharaohs*, is a pushy, opinionated woman, who consistently rushes into danger, because she is convinced she can do the job—any job—better than anyone else.

There are other reasons why the heroine might not want to leave Castle Grimly, but I think that gives you the idea. Let's proceed to point B.

B. *The heroine cannot leave.*

1. She is physically isolated—by terrain, or even bad weather.

She may be on an island and the villain has destroyed all the boats. Or perhaps a flood has devastated the countryside, so that roads, telephones, etc., are unusable. One of my heroines found herself in a distant part of the Scottish Highlands, with a blizzard raging, just when she had (belatedly, I admit) made up her mind to leave. Clearly, it is easier to arrange such isolation if you set your novel in an earlier century, when methods of transportation and communication were more primitive. But even in a modern setting it can be done, if you invent an earthquake or volcanic eruption, or if you have placed your heroine in a remote village in Greece or Africa.

2. She is isolated by social or political circumstances.

In the modern romantic suspense novel, this can be achieved by placing the girl in the remote foreign village mentioned above. Few places in this day and age are so physically remote that there is not a telephone or a village constable available, but if the heroine is unfamiliar with the language—if she has no local sponsors who can vouch for her sanity and her honesty—if she is in some part of the world where women lack prestige—under such circumstances it is possible to construct a plot where she must rely on her own wits and strength.

3. She is isolated by legal barriers.

The most conspicuous examples of such restrictions are the legal inequities affecting women in England and America during the early Victorian period. During most of the nineteenth century, women could not vote, hold office, or attend professional schools or universities. More to the point for the writer of romantic suspense fiction is the fact that they could not own property or get a divorce, even in cases of physical abuse.

The classic example of such mistreatment can be seen in *The Woman in White*—my favorite romantic suspense novel—by Wilkie Collins. His heroine was vulnerable because English law gave her husband absolute control over her property and her person.

4. She is imprisoned—locked in her room or in the dungeons of Castle Grimly.

This probably won't work for an entire book. In *The Count of Monte Cristo,* Dumas described at great length his hero's attempts to break out of prison; but no matter how ingenious you are, it is unlikely that you can sustain interest in this device for three hundred pages. However, I would love to see someone pull it off.

5. She is too shy, intimidated, or neurotic to fight back to try to escape.

Personality disorders of this sort are common, even in this liberated age. I fear, however, that in this case truth is too unconvincing for fiction. Readers are not inclined to sympathize with such an insipid female. The primary weakness of *Rebecca*, one of the great romantic suspense novels, is that the shy, unworldly heroine arouses more irritation than pity.

One step removed from this problem, but related to it, is the plot development of another form of romantic suspense story, in which the heroine, instead of investigating the tower where the body lies, or its equivalent, takes to her heels and flees the villain. It is the feminine version of the "chase" story, and here, as in the first type, the difficulty is one of motivation: why does she run from danger into danger instead of stopping at the nearest police station?

I. *She loses her wits and runs off in panic.*

Forget this one. It may be what you or I would do, but it is not acceptable behavior for a heroine. Not only is it lazy technique, but it smacks of male chauvinism—"you know how women are; they lose their heads in a crisis." Modern women readers won't buy this, nor should they.

Mind you, a number of famous male heroes have succumbed to this very weakness. In John Buchan's masterpiece, *The Thirty-Nine Steps*, the hero, Richard Hannay takes off in mindless flight after finding a body in his sitting room. Hannay is a strong macho male and a member of the sacred upper class; his explanation of why the murdered man happened to be in his flat might have raised a few eyebrows at Scotland Yard, but could not possibly have resulted in his arrest. Any reader who has followed his marvelous adventures has no cause for complaint, but a heroine who behaved in such a rattle-brained fashion would undoubtedly be blasted by the critics. Buchan gets away with it because of the grace and style of his writing (and perhaps because critics are more tolerant of irrational behavior in a hero than in a heroine?), but unless you are able to replicate Buchan's strengths, you should not copy his weaknesses.

II. *Her credibility is in doubt; the police will not believe her.*

a. She herself is a suspect in a murder or bank heist, or whatever crime you chose to invent.

The circumstantial evidence against her must be strong, or she will be guilty of point I (above)—mindless flight. It's not hard to set up such a plot. Perhaps the real murderer has framed her, planting the blood-stained knife in her lingerie drawer, or luring her to the scene of the crime by means of a spurious message. Alternatively, she may be fortuitously involved because of a strong motive (and no alibi) or because of a history of mental instability, a previous criminal record, or the like. The literature teems with examples.

b. The reason she is being pursued is not known even to her; she can't possibly hope to convince the police.

Again, there are two sub-variants. The first may arise from a pre-existing fact of which the heroine is not aware; for example, she is the true heir to millionaire Uncle Donald's estate. Or else her danger stems from what I call the "initiating coincidence" that sets a suspense plot moving. My heroines are always running into people who thrust mysterious parcels or cryptic messages into their unwilling hands. My novel *Legend in Green Velvet* began with a case of mistaken identity. The conspirator, a rather confused elderly gentleman, passed his message to the wrong woman. I tried to use a variant of the chase technique by having the heroine pursue the conspirator, to try to give him back his parcel. In the meantime, she is herself pursued by assorted villains who also want the parcel. Though my heroine quite properly calls the police when her room is ransacked, it does not occur to her or to them that the innocent-looking parcel can be responsible for the break-in.

c. The events that convince her she is in danger are so preposterous no one would credit them.

I like this trick because I like to invent preposterous circumstances. When my middle-aged heroine in *Copenhagen Connection* disappears, presumably kidnapped, her friends cannot convince the police she needs help, because the ransom note does not demand money; it asks for "Margaret's bathrobe."

d. The pursuer has the law on his side.

Mary Stewart—who does the modern romantic suspense novel as well as any writer in the business—used this in *Madam, Will You Talk?* The presumed villain was the father of the child Stewart's heroine wanted to protect. She had excellent reasons for believing him to be a threat to the child, but she had no legal right to interfere.

e. The villains are in such hot pursuit that the girl doesn't have time to stop and explain the situation.

This works best when combined with several of the other points mentioned. The more unbelievable the circumstances, the longer it will take the heroine to make a convincing case. The farther she is from home, the less likely it is that her story will be believed.

f. She has reason to suspect that the police official or the entire police force is involved in the crime.

Unhappily, this is a convincing argument these days, when the average newspaper reader is only too well acquainted with tales of police corruption or brutality. Again, it works well when combined with other factors, such as that of isolation; a woman in a foreign country whose legal code is strange to her may be reluctant to trust the local sheriff. Or perhaps she has observed the sheriff in friendly conversation with her pursuer. . . .

The girl *must* go to the tower where the body lies. She *must* be in danger. What counts is *why* she goes.

7

"HAD-I-BUT-KNOWN": HOW TO USE IT IN PLOTTING ROMANTIC SUSPENSE

by Barbara Mertz

Pseudonyms: Barbara Michaels
Elizabeth Peters

Imprints: Dodd, Mead
Congdon & Weed

PART 2

IT might seem that clues are not essential to a romantic suspense novel, at least not to the same degree as in the straight detective story. In some types of suspense fiction, such as the chase tale, clues may be dispensed with. The reader doesn't care who the villains are or why they are in pursuit; he is interested only in the protagonist's efforts to escape. But in many romantic suspense stories, there is a mystery to be solved or a plot to be uncovered before the heroine can relax—in the arms of the hero or elsewhere, as she prefers. Bright readers like to exercise their wits as well as their emotions. They know, when they read my books, that there will be a happy ending (so far, I haven't written any other kind). But if they can anticipate the method by which that ending is to be achieved, they will, I believe, be more pleased with themselves and with me. They

51

have a right to expect clues that will enable them to work out at least part of the answer; and if the story is not to come to a premature end, those clues must be suppressed or ignored by the heroine. The writer's challenge is to invent valid reasons for the girl's failure to employ those clues to protect herself. Here are a few examples of some of the clues employed in successful romantic suspense fiction and how to deal with them.

A. *The classic clue,* used in all forms of mystery fiction, including, upon occasion, romantic suspense.

1. Facts or objects deliberately suppressed by the heroine, thus obfuscating the mystery: the bloodstained handkerchief, the murder weapon, the initialled cigarette case under the body.

Do try to avoid these. They have been overused to the point of caricature, and they never were very convincing. If the heroine really suspects that her lover has slaughtered kindly old Grandma Smith, she has no business trying to protect him, and if she is sure he is innocent, she ought to realize that she may be making matters worse: The concealed object may contain a clue to the real murderer. If you must use this hoary old device, at least make sure the girl destroys the evidence completely: Be certain the bloodstained handkerchief is totally consumed in the library fireplace, or that the gun won't turn up again under even more damning circumstances. She should also check to see that the library door is closed and that none of the servants is peeking through the keyhole.

2. Clues that are overlooked or misinterpreted.

This is the standard method of planting evidence. The difficulty is that it must be hidden so neatly that even an intelligent heroine will logically overlook it. A number of the methods used in the straight detective story to accomplish this can be used successfully in romantic suspense novels, too. Here are a few I favor.

The easiest method is to admit the reader into the confidence of someone other than the protagonist—perhaps the villain himself. In *The Chocolate Cobweb*, by Charlotte Armstrong, the reader actually watches the murderer manipulating the mechanism by which the heroine is to be annihilated. No one else in the house knows about the device, so hero and heroine cannot be blamed for failing to anticipate its use, and the suspense of the reader is heightened as he watches the girl unwittingly walk toward her doom.

Comment by an omniscient narrator (the author) is another way of planting a clue that is known to the reader but is justifiably ignored by the heroine. I did this in *Black Rainbow*, where it seemed particularly appropriate since the book is a Victorian thriller; the technique is typical of the writing of that period. "It was not Jane's fault that she missed the real significance of the incident. She was now too far removed from the world in which such ideas still lingered, passed on from father to son and mother to daughter, fading slowly with the passage of the centuries but ready to leap up like a smoldering fire when fresh kindling is added." The purplish prose and the hints of uncanny peril are in keeping with Victorian melodrama, and are typical HIBK technique.

The most difficult and most craftsmanlike method of planting an obscure clue is to tell a straight story, without interpolations from minor characters or the author, and to bury the evidence. For example:

a) The casual comment. The pertinent statement, seemingly irrelevant, but actually vital to the solution, is buried by hiding it in a mass of verbiage. I find this easy to do since my characters are hopelessly loquacious; they talk all the time. In *Street of the Five Moons,* my heroine missed an essential clue—an admission, by the hero, that he had entertained various ladies in his hotel room—because she was jealous; they were arguing; and the villains were pounding at the door. Anyone might be excused for being distracted under such circumstances. Later, when things had calmed down, she remembered the remark and was able to deduce the identity of the Master Criminal.

b) The esoteric clue—information so obscure that only a specialist in the subject can interpret its significance. This is contemptible. I have often made use of it. But don't underestimate your readers; a few of them will spot the clue and will pat themselves on the back for their cleverness. Readers of my supernatural romances have learned to be suspicious of any group of nine people: It may turn out to be a witches' coven. And if St. Johnswort turns up in the narrative, look out for a ghostly attack on the heroine.

You can give the impression that you are playing fair if you interpret the esoteric clue as you plant it. In *Curse of the Pharaohs,* an ancient Egyptian fairy tale points directly to the identity of the killer; although I analyzed the story in painstaking detail, its specific application eluded most readers.

B. *Clues, dire hints and portents particularly applicable to the romantic suspense novel.*

1. Concealing the identity of the hero.

This is important, not only to the romance, but to the suspense. The actions of male characters may be deliberately ambiguous, and if the heroine trusts the wrong man, she may be asking for a sojourn in the dungeons of Castle Grimly. I am beginning to suspect I do not hide clues of this nature as well as I ought; my hero is only too often the man the heroine particularly dislikes at the beginning of the book. Such insight need not destroy the reader's enjoyment of the story, but it is essential that the writer account logically for behavior that may lead the heroine into a mistaken identification.

In my novel *Witch,* I had two separate cases of mistaken identity. The real hero of the book departed in chapter one and did not re-enter the story until the moment of crisis, several hundred pages later. It was necessary to remind the reader of his existence, so I had the heroine stare dreamily at his picture, write and receive letters from him, and so on. The other candidate for the position of hero was on the spot, being charming to the heroine. Not only was he the villain, he was a consummate villain, one of the nastiest I have ever invented, and one of his victims had to appear villainous until virtually the end of the book. The real villain committed several of the criminal acts attributed to the victim, whose reputation he had carefully destroyed. Other situations were set up by the villain in such a way that the victim's acts were misinterpreted by witnesses. One of the points I wanted to make was the degree to which preconceptions and prejudices influence the interpretation of a given act.

One writer who deals magnificently with this problem is Dorothy Dunnett. In every book of the series featuring Francis Crawford of Lymond, Francis starts out looking like a man with no redeeming characteristics whatever. He sets fire to the family home, attacks his sister-in-law, and tries to kill his brother—and that's all in the first volume. By the end of each book Dunnett has not only explained Lymond's apparent villainy, but has turned him into a persecuted hero. Her books are not true romantic suspense, but any writer who wants to use the villain-hero confusion to enhance the drama cannot do better than study Dunnett's methods.

2. The classic, flat-out "Had-I-But-Known" label, which identifies the statement in question as vital to the solution. In effect, the writer is saying, "Here it is—what do you think I'm going to do with it?"

This differs from the clue that is planted by the omniscient narrator in that it is voiced by the protagonist, who speaks in the first person. There are two things to avoid like the plague in using this device. First, don't use the phrase "had I but known," unless you do it satirically. It has become a form of satire in itself and cannot be taken seriously by the reader. Second, avoid the obvious, "Had I but known the smoking pistol was the murder weapon, I would never have hidden it in my knitting bag." Only an idiot could miss the implications of a smoking pistol at the scene of a murder.

At one point in *Borrower of the Night,* when my detective heroine finds a peculiar little golden image, "a dark and elusive memory stirred unpleasantly in the back of my mind—stirred and subsided, like a slimy thing in a swamp." The words "had I but known" are not used, but they are implicit—and the reader knows this object is going to be an essential clue. The old master, Wilkie Collins, was particularly good at this sort of thing. Here is the comment of the family lawyer, after he has drawn up the heroine's marriage settlement, in *The Woman in White:*

"No daughter of mine should have been married to any man alive under such a settlement as I was compelled to make for Laura Fairlie." This is HIBK at its best and most effective—setting a tone of foreboding, of incipient and unavoidable danger.

"Had I but known" is a lament we all utter, only too often, in the course of normal life. Had I but known the cat was going to jump onto the mantel I wouldn't have left my favorite Sèvres vase up there. Had I but known the man standing on the corner was an escaped thief, I wouldn't have neglected to lock the car. . . . None of us is omniscient; all of us are careless and unobservant at times. If the writer can play on this human weakness, he gains strongly in reader sympathy and reader identification. However, people tend to forget their mistakes; they don't want to identify with average idiots like themselves (or me). It is perilously easy for a writer to go too far in depending on human weakness to excuse his protagonist's mistakes. The feeling he wants to evoke in the reader is not "I wouldn't be stupid enough to do a thing like that," but rather, "That's just what I would have done," or "I do that sort of thing myself when I get rattled." So don't avoid the HIBK tricks. Use them correctly, and you will acquire a whole boxful of tools that can increase the effectiveness of your romantic suspense novel.

8

POINT OF VIEW IN ROMANTIC FICTION

by Diana Brown

Imprints: New American Library
St. Martin's Press

"ONCE upon a time," begin our favorite fairy tales, before going on to describe characters and events. Fairy tales, most of which are, at their very best, love stories—"Cinderella," "Beauty and the Beast," "Sleeping Beauty"—remain happily and steadfastly still with us, in their original forms as well as in recurring ideas in stories and novels down through the centuries. They grew from that ancient oral tradition, passed on from one generation to another, that regarded life simply, but from the view of an all-seeing, all-knowing eye.

Over the ages fiction has changed, evolved, refined; theme, character, plot, style, are more carefully considered in the translation of inspiration into finished work. But from Samuel Richardson, father of the English romantic novel, to contemporary novelists, perhaps no matter has absorbed writers more than that of point of view.

How can a story best be told? Through whose eyes should it unfold? How much freedom does the writer require to enter the minds of the characters? Should the plot be revealed through the eyes of all, or only some of them; through the main protagonists, or perhaps from one only? Does the story require the intimacy, the immediacy of first-person narration, or the greater detachment and wider scope of third? Should the novelist himself play narrator (as Somerset Maugham often did with considerable success)? Does an omniscient narrator provide too much distance? Most nineteenth-century writers didn't think so, nor did Tolstoy hesitate to intrude upon that god-like view with his own moralizing. Would a dual view be preferable, or could a diary or letters best serve—a device Samuel Richardson used in *Pamela* and *Clarissa*, and skillfully revived by Elizabeth Forsythe Hailey in *A Woman of Independent Means*?

Although the main choice lies between first- and third-person narration, there are nuances within each. Richard Yates successfully used both in his novel *A Good School*, beginning and ending it in the first person, with the main body of the novel in the third.

The matter of viewpoint was one on which I pondered when I first began writing fiction; it still remains an important consideration. While I believe the choice of narrator should be made early in the creation of a work, from my own experience I know that no decision is irrevocable. Sometimes only after a work is underway does the right point of view emerge: A writer may begin with an omniscient view only to discover himself moving into the intricacies of the mind of one character above all others, seeing events unfold through *that* character's eyes and *that* character's eyes only.

This is precisely what happened to me in writing my

first novel, *The Emerald Necklace.* My intention had been to tell the story of its hero, Etienne Lambert, a man living in early nineteenth-century England, who has experienced and overcome difficulties of illegitimate birth and poverty, and in a land of inherited wealth and power, has succeeded entirely through his own efforts. Etienne has the fortune—or misfortune—to fall in love with Leonora Fordyce, a titled young lady, spoiled, flighty, and arrogant, a lady of the society that rejects him, a society that he, in turn, despises.

Before I was very far into Etienne's story, however, though it remained and still is *his* story, I began to see it through the eyes of Leonora, a vain social butterfly who finds herself married to a man for whom she feels neither love nor sympathy. Hers I found to be a splendid and devious mind through which to create my story and to observe an admirable man from her narrow, yet increasingly broadening point of view.

Because *The Emerald Necklace* was Etienne's story, it was important to enlist the reader's enthusiasm and empathy for him, though this had to be done from Leonora's disinterested viewpoint. Since he is the man who is to turn her from a shallow, unsympathetic girl into a thinking, acting woman, his integrity and worth had to be shown through his words and actions, as observed and described by her. Although he realizes that his young wife does not love him, Etienne is willing to love and protect her, but he risks her further dislike by insisting that she assume responsibilities that are rightfully hers. Thus, when Leonora deliberately loses a large sum of money gambling, despite being told by her husband that he will not be held accountable for such debts, he insists she settle the matter herself. To do so, she is forced to visit a pawnshop in Cheapside to dispose of her emerald necklace, after which she concludes:

> Despite the mortification of the moment, I had an odd sense of pride. It was the first matter I had ever handled on my own.

And it is at this point that growth and change begin for Leonora, her first-person voice portraying her maturing viewpoint. My second novel, *Come Be My Love*, was the story of Alexandra Cox-Neville from girl to adult and was never conceived except in her voice. The first line of the novel sets its tone: "I fell in love with Darius Wentworth when I was twelve."

In *Come Be My Love* I felt it important early in the novel to describe Alexandra's appearance, because I am convinced that faces reveal character. Thus, in the first chapter, the reader looks over Alexandra's shoulder as she gazes into a mirror, disappointed that the reflection there may not be sufficiently attractive to win the approval of her new-found love:

> My eyes were almost exactly the same brown as my hair; mother called them expressive, but I thought they were too far apart for beauty. They were large, that I liked, but so, too, was my mouth, there was nothing of the rosebud about that. I smiled at myself and it became positively expansive, not at all what I wanted even if it did make me look very happy.

The first-person narration in *The Emerald Necklace* and *Come Be My Love* helped the reader to know and understand their heroines completely, yet there remained the difficulty of describing events essential to the plot but beyond the narrator's knowledge. For example, in *The Emerald Necklace*, when Leonora's friend

Phoebe (whom she suspects of having won the affections of her estranged husband) unexpectedly becomes engaged, the explanation of this turn of events is given in Phoebe's answer to a congratulatory letter immediately dispatched by a mystified Leonora.

In *Come Be My Love,* Alexandra runs away from her own wedding, yet rather than leave to the reader's imagination the important scene of the church filled with guests, both the reader and Alexandra were enlightened by Paul, her brother, who was present:

> "Well, it wasn't exactly comfortable. I counted nine times that the organist played 'O Perfect Love' until either he, or the organ, or both gave out."

And so on, until the jilted bridegroom announced himself famished, adding:

> ". . . even though there's not going to be a wedding, I can't see why all that good food should go to waste."

It was my intention in my next novel, *A Debt of Honour,* to follow the path of my previous books, using first-person viewpoint to tell the tale of its redoubtable Scottish heroine, Fiona Guthrie, who is left in straitened circumstances to maintain her ancestral abbey, a home for which she would give anything, even herself. A problem arose, however, when I realized the importance of establishing the hero, Peter Chalmsforth, as a man of worth, although his initial meeting with Fiona shows him in a less than favorable light. I therefore shifted from the first-person view of Fiona, to third, and started the novel through Peter's eyes, then changed to Fiona's. From then on, it moved back and forth to show their growing love for one another. Though there are occasional insights into the minds of others, *A Debt of*

Honour is a novel of dual narration in the third-person. This allowed far greater leeway in the telling, far more detachment. Freed from the constriction of the single viewpoint, the writing was in many ways easier, in many ways more fun—but it was also less intense.

St. Martin's Summer, the love story of Josephina Trafford, a gentlewoman farmer raising merino sheep, and her neighbor, Conniston Venables, also features Josephina's petulant and obstinate mother, a selfless as well as a selfish sister, a belligerent squire and his good lady, a plodding suitor, all of whose minds at some point I wanted to enter. For this reason, I chose to tell the story from multiple points of view. Thus while the locale of *St. Martin's Summer,* a Devon village, is more limited than those of my other novels, its angle of narration is wider by far.

Telling a story solely from the point of view of the hero and heroine, requiring one or the other to be "on stage" at all times, may place a burden upon movement and may even lead to monotony. They must, of course, bear the weight of a plot that is, after all, their love story, and it is important to elicit empathy and understanding for them, but a change of viewpoint—even to that of less estimable characters—can provide relief and contrast.

In *The Sandalwood Fan,* the paths of protagonists military hero Charles Mortimer and widow Penelope Bransom cross; they convey their quite different backgrounds, each in turn from his or her own viewpoint, and in doing so, reveal much of their personalities. The reader follows their changing regard for one another as an affection begins to develop between them, setting their romance in motion.

The course of true love, in novels at least, can rarely be allowed to run smoothly, and I show many other characters, broadly classified as "villains," contriving to thwart their growing love. To make these minor, though nonetheless important, characters and their motivation believable, it became important, at times, to relate through their eyes not only their view of themselves but also their view of others. Though their appetites might border on gluttony and their thrift on cupidity, they had to be entirely human so they would not become the moustache-twirling caricatures of melodrama.

It was possible to convey "comic villainy" by a single trait—the inveterate though often malevolent gossip of a chaperone, or the knavery of a Cockney in the pungent rhyming slang he uses—but the real villainy of the inheritor of Penelope's husband's estate; the vacillations of her weak brother; and the hypocrisy of a supposed philanthropist, could be clearly understood only through their views of the events. Misapprehensions may abound in the plot, but they should not remain long in the mind of the reader; *The Sandalwood Fan*, after all, is a love story, not a mystery.

I have tried, and continue to try different ways of telling a tale, from the multiple view of *The Sandalwood Fan* and *St. Martin's Summer,* to the dual third-person of *A Debt of Honour,* and the first-person narration of *Come Be My Love* and *The Emerald Necklace.* All have been challenging, and in each case ultimately I have been satisfied with the angle of narration I have chosen.

Careful attention to point of view can not only improve a work, it can, and has, made the difference between a good novel and a great one. Could *Vanity Fair* have been written in the first person and still conveyed its great panorama of life? Or would *Jane Eyre* have continued to live in the romantic imagination had it been told from a detached omniscient view? I think not.

In all discussion of first- versus third-person narration and their varied nuances, it is important not to forget the all-important second person, the *you,* the reader to whom the tale is being transmitted. Writing is communication. If the angle of narration in any way restricts full disclosure, or is either too intense for the material or too distant to convey vital emotions, the story's impact may be lost, or it may simply fail to come alive to the reader who may close the book without caring about the outcome—or else may finish it only to be left with a sense of dissatisfaction.

9

WRITING THE ROMANTIC NOVEL YOU'D LIKE TO READ

by Margaret Chittenden

Pseudonym: Rosalind Carson

Imprint: Harlequin Superromances

I WRITE about a very serious subject—love. To my amazement, I've discovered there are people who look upon the writing of romance as frivolous. This is far from the truth. There is nothing frivolous about love. Love is important to every member of the human race—it is one of the most complex emotions there is, and one of the most fascinating to explore in fiction.

One advantage in writing romantic novels is that you can draw on your own experience. You can't always do that with murder mysteries or police procedurals, but all of us know something about love. All of us have had some romance in our lives, and even if passion is not something we experience every day, we can at least depend on memory.

Today is boom time for romantic novels. If you look in the bookstores, you'll see rack upon rack of them,

66

appealing to readers from teen age to the very, very adult. When I decided to try romance writing, I read as many romances as I could. To my horror, I found I didn't really enjoy many of them, but I could see that they all had certain essential ingredients in common. It seemed to me, therefore, that as long as I kept these in mind, there was no reason for me not to be able to write the kind of book I'd like to read.

So far, this method has worked very well for me. Let's look at these necessary ingredients and see how they work in writing a romance novel. I'll begin with setting.

My first decision in writing a romance novel is, where is it going to take place? Preferably, the setting should be interesting, even glamorous. I live in the suburbs now, but at heart I am of the city. I love galleries, huge department stores, luxury hotels, museums, historic buildings, gourmet food, and, since I am writing to please myself first, I usually set my books in or near a major city. Other writers seem to feel at home in the jungle or desert or on a tropical island, but since such places make me think of snakes or sunstroke or insects that bite in the night, I don't feel capable of making them appealing to a romance reader.

If possible, I visit my chosen location; if not, I research the place thoroughly until I know every alley, every important landmark. I want to know what the weather is like, the smell of the air, the food specialties, the people, the *personality* of the city—the characteristics and elements that make that city different from other cities.

From this research comes the background of the novel. When I used Edinburgh, Scotland as the setting of one of my novels, I settled on the annual Edinburgh Music Festival for its background. For *Song of Desire* I chose London and Stratford-on-Avon. Most of the background is theatrical. The fact that I enjoy music and drama influenced these decisions.

As soon as I have the background in mind, the next ingredient is easy. Characters begin forming in my mind. The musical background brought forth a famous conductor, a composer, a violinist. In *Song of Desire*, with its theatrical background, the hero is a Shakespearean actor, another character is a drama critic, another heads an arts foundation. And so on.

My main female character, the heroine, is always an American. She is going to the place I have chosen. Why? "Why?" is always my first question. The answer to that first "why?" starts my plot moving and raises up other "whys" to keep the plot building.

In my romance novel reading, I noticed that in the first chapter, the heroine usually had a confrontation with the hero under circumstances that would generate conflict as well as attraction. Conflict is as necessary in a romance as it is in any other kind of fiction; perhaps more so. The road to true love does not run smoothly.

In plotting a work of fiction, I try to visualize my characters—though they are not yet fully realized—against their background and setting and watch what they do. Usually, they start talking to me, prodded by a "why" here and a "how" there. After a while, they start talking and reacting to each other, and I write down what they say and do. As my characters develop, my plot builds; as my plot builds, my characters develop. It's a symbiotic relationship.

I try to avoid stock characters. I imagine almost anyone could give me a quick description of the typical romance novel hero: over six feet tall, lean and muscular, or lean and lithe. Probably dark-haired, usually rich, grim perhaps, or brooding. Nowadays the hero still has to be physically attractive, but he doesn't have to be a cliché. Again, I go back to my own preferences. What kind of man attracts me? Not the macho type who grabs the heroine by the wrist and pins her down on the sofa or bed in almost every scene. He's rather outdated anyway. I like a man who has a sense of humor, compassion, even humility. He might want to seduce the heroine, but he would never, ever, use force. I give him some flaws, but I let him, on occasion, speak nicely to the heroine. In short, I try to make him a real person.

I want my heroine to be a real person, too. Some of the heroines I read about seem a bit dim-witted to me. I can't imagine why any man would fall in love with such a silly woman. My heroine is the kind of woman I would like to be. She is usually tall and physically healthy. She jogs, or swims. She is striking and has a mind of her own. She is intelligent. She is a career woman. She may tremble a little from time to time, but who among us does not?

I try to avoid trite situations as well as people. I've lost count of the times I've read a scene in which the heroine appears in front of the hero clad only in a diaphanous nightgown. She does not usually realize this until two or three pages of dialogue later, *then* she remembers, but it's too late. I will confess that I've done variations on this theme, though. In my novel, *This Dark Enchantment,* the heroine often practiced ballet exercises in the basement recreation room. She wore a leotard, of course, which is not the most concealing of garments. And, of course, the hero happened upon her. (Well, no, not *happened;* he had a reason for being there—I try to motivate *everything* in my novels.)

One problem I have in writing romantic novels is that

I run out of words to describe a romantic scene. I certainly don't want to use "tumultuous" or "magnetic" or "electrical" all the time, though some writers do. I've found that it is possible to come up with original descriptions, if I keep the background and characters clearly in mind. In *Song of Desire,* for instance, my characters quote Shakespeare once in a while. I also use metaphors and similes, though not too often: They can get to be too much of a good thing. I also use earlier experiences of my heroine as a way of revealing how she feels in the present. Here's an example from *Song of Desire.*

> She was reminded suddenly of a time one of those athletic boyfriends of hers had persuaded her to try sky-diving. She was suffering now from the same terrified exhilaration she'd experienced when she had to separate herself from the airplane.

While I'm writing, I try to bear in mind another requirement of the genre: There should be *tension* between the hero and heroine at all times. Even when they are getting along with each other, even just walking along a street. And the tension should build. Occasionally it should peak. It must be there when the man and woman are in the midst of a crowd, or when they are alone together—when they are quarreling and when they are making love.

I also try to create suspense even in minor ways. The main suspense of course is—will they or won't they? One small example of minor suspense: At one point in *Song of Desire,* Jason invites Vicki to go out to dinner with him. "I want to talk to you about something," he says. He looks rather furtively around the room. "Away from here," he adds. Vicki is filled with curiosity and a certain amount of nervousness, wondering what he wants to talk about that can't be discussed on the spot. The reader, I hope, will then follow through the next ten pages to find out what Jason is up to. Remember that if you create suspense like that, you have to follow through and make it important to the resolution of the novel; you can't let the reader down.

Though there may be subplots, the central story in a romance novel is the romance between the hero and heroine and the rocky road they travel before promising to love happily ever after.

Not all of today's romantic novels restrict themselves to "pure" love. Many of these are no longer subject to an iron law that says that young women must be virgins before marriage. But modern heroines are *never* promiscuous, and they are still expected to be eternally faithful after marriage.

Obviously, the hero and heroine aren't falling in love in a vacuum. They are going to have love scenes of varying degrees of intensity—and these have to be set somewhere. Again, I go back to my research on setting and background. In Quebec City, the setting for *This Dark Enchantment*, I once watched the Dominion Day fireworks and parade of boats, from the Plains of Abraham. For the novel, I dressed that experience up a bit—the heroine watches from the deck of a yacht—with the hero. (And incidentally, suffers from a touch of *mal de mer*—more romantic than seasickness. The hero is a French-Canadian doctor, so it's believable for him to escort the heroine to one of the cabins, to make her more "comfortable," which of course provides a good opportunity for dalliance.) In *Song of Desire*, I used my own experience of punting on a river, which in reality was hair-raising as well as hilarious, but in the novel, it became another opportunity for romance.

Everyone's experiences and preferences are unique. If a writer romanticizes them, he or she will always be able to create original scenes. It might seem deceitful, perhaps, to present life in such romantic terms, but I think most people read these books because they want to feel that life *sometimes* works out the way it should—or the way they'd like it to.

It's very easy to write mediocre romantic novels, but it's not necessary for romances to be mediocre. I hesitate to admit that I do a lot of work on my novels; I'm always afraid someone will read one of my novels and say, "Is this the *best* she can do?" But it is. I polish and revise and agonize over every book until it's as good as I can make it—until it pleases *me.* I especially check to see that the viewpoint is consistent, that I'm never guilty of writing something like: "Sonia's emerald eyes glittered in her exquisite face," when I'm writing from Sonia's viewpoint. A sentence like that would put the reader off Sonia for life.

Writing romance is fun—it's fantasy time every day—it's escape—it's entertainment. It's also very hard work. Or it should be. I would like to encourage other writers to *respect* their craft, whatever they are writing, and give it their best. The results will please them. Surely, every writer should enjoy reading his or her own books. That's one of the major rewards of being a writer.

10

REGENCY ROMANCE ROMP

by Joan Aiken

Imprints: Delacorte Press
Doubleday & Co.
Warner Books

FIRST, what is a Regency romance? Second, why choose to write one? Third, how are they written? And, fourth, who reads them?

I shall try to answer these questions.

Nobody can profess a knowledge of the Regency field lacking a degree of familiarity with the novels of Georgette Heyer, who, if she cannot be said to have invented the genre, at least gave the twentieth-century version such a personal touch that "school of Georgette Heyer" will probably remain a defining term for decades to come. But let us first take a look at earlier sources.

Pedantically speaking, many romances published during the reign of the Prince Regent, George IV of England as he ultimately became, constituted the first examples of the genre. Of course, novelists who were alive and writing during this period, between 1811 and 1820 (or 1830 when George IV died), felt free to set their stories in other, or indefinite periods, as novelists always do. However, present-day writers attempting a Regency romance usually stay within those dates.

What must, without any doubt, be taken as required reading for would-be Regency writers are the novels of Jane Austen, who constitutes all on her own the third or classic school of Regency fiction. Of course, these works have passed beyond any single classification and are for all time and all readers. But they also give one of the most faithful pictures that we have of Regency society, and I do not believe that any writer aspiring to enter the Regency field can even consider putting paper in type-writer without first making a close study of the Austen novels. The style, settings, details on every page of contemporary habits, speech, thought, morality, finance, reading matter, what was considered acceptable behavior and what was not, make them an essential source of period material. Fanny Burney is almost equally important. I myself, when writing in this genre, refresh myself with frequent dips into their books, so as to keep my ear tuned to contemporary rhythms of speech and flavor of vocabulary. My sister (the novelist Jane Aiken Hodge, a specialist in this period) has gone further and possesses a copy of Samuel Johnson's Dictionary; she checks all doubtful words to make sure that they would have been in use at that time and are not later and anachronistic arrivals. "Upset," for instance, meaning distressed, would be anachronistic—the correct eighteenth-century usage would be "overset."

Needless to say, reading lives of contemporary figures, such as Richard Brinsley Sheridan, Beau Brummel, George IV himself, memoirs and letters of the time, such as those of Byron or Prince Pückler-Muskau, contemporary journals like *The Gentleman's Magazine* and *La Belle Assemblee,* or present-day accounts of the period like T.H. White's *The Age of Scandal,* will all help to fill out the background.

It is certainly due to Georgette Heyer that the Regency novel has such an established place in public popularity at the moment, and since readers' expectations are formed on the model she set, it is worth making a study of some of the forty-odd novels she wrote in this genre. She herself, apparently, looked on them as pure potboilers and greatly preferred her own detective fiction, but there can be no question that she took considerable pains with her Regencies and acquired her facts by much careful period research; rather *too* much, indeed, toward the end of her career. The later novels tend to be an indigestible mass of detail about clothes, food, carriages, fashion, with whole paragraphs of slang. Contrariwise, the early novels, such as *Powder and Patch, The Black Moth, The Masqueraders,* are action-packed, but rather too swashbuckling and full of "tushery" and "quothery" for my taste. In my opinion Heyer's middle period, from *The Convenient Marriage* onward, constitutes her best work. As pure entertainment, for charm, humor, ingenuity of plot, and just the right amount of period detail, I believe these middle novels can hardly be faulted.

The usual theme (like that of Jane Austen) is simple: a rather hard-up, though well-born, heroine falls in love with and in the end marries a well-born, rich hero. Occasionally the heroine has money of her own (as in *Regency Buck, Bath Tangle, A Civil Contract*). Then among her difficulties is that of weeding out the fortune-hunters. There is a fair amount of physical adventure:

duels, highwaymen, attempted murder for inheritance, espionage, and smuggling are complications with which resourceful heroines have to deal. The later novels rely more on social comedy—accidental or impulsive deceptions and the consequent misunderstandings arising. An impoverished girl pretends to be rich out of pique at the hero's snubbing her; a rich hero, in order to tease his snobbish relatives, pretends to be poor; a couple pretends to be engaged so that the heroine can escape from her guardian and come to London to husband-hunt. Or there are predicament-plots: A heroine applying for a post as governess arrives at the wrong house and is swiftly married off by the enterprising hero to his dying villainous cousin in order to avoid inheritance problems.

The plots are not far from those of eighteenth-century comedy—Oliver Goldsmith's *She Stoops to Conquer* and Sheridan's *The Rivals*—and a study of that field is not a bad indoctrination for Regency writers. One of Heyer's very best middle-period novels is *Sylvester*, in which the heroine, affronted by the hero's haughty ways (Regency heroes are nearly always haughty, an amalgam of Darcy, from *Pride and Prejudice*, and Rochester, from *Jane Eyre*), satirizes him in an anonymous novel and subsequently falls in love with him. The turns and twists of this plot are embellished with some of Heyer's best comedy characters: an irascible grandmother; a silly, self-indulgent sister-in-law; an empty-headed dandy, Sir Nugent Fotherby, with a splendid line of Regency slang; and a country squire who thinks more of his horses than his daughters.

Some critics have complained that all Heyer's characters speak the same language, but I think this shows the lack of a perceptive ear. The changing dialogue seems to me one of the great pleasures in a Heyer novel. Heroines talk very correctly, with an eighteenth-century elegance of phrase: "The most shocking flirt in town, I am persuaded. He does very well for one's entertainment, but the female who receives his advances seriously will be destined, I fear, to sad disappointment."

Younger brothers break out in Regency slang: "I ain't so high in the instep!" And dandies like Sir Nugent Fotherby have a line all their own: "I was surprised. You might say I was betwattled."

It is not always important, in some historical novels, to use period forms of speech, and I do not think one needs to be fanatical about it. It is very much a matter of opinion. If period setting and characters are strong and convincing, then there should be no need for archaisms. A fairly plain, formal speech without modern slang should be sufficient to create an historical atmosphere. But in the Regency novel, I would make an exception to this rule. The language and vocabulary of that epoch— so clear, precise, elegant, agreeable to the ear—is a delight in itself. The language is, for me, one of the chief pleasures and justifications for writing Regency novels: a wish to refresh oneself by using a more gracious style. It is like putting on a long skirt for evening wear: It immediately gives a grace and dignity lacking in everyday usage.

Consider a few of Jane Austen's run-of-the-mill sentences: "I do not dispute his virtues; but I do not like his careless air." "Vanity was the beginning and end of Sir Walter Elliot's character." "She had nothing against her, but her husband, and her conscience." "It was on the wedding day of this beloved friend that Emma first sat in mournful thought of any continuance."

Another reason for writing Regency novels is that the

plots are such fun and so civilized. Compared to our novels today, when a plot in itself is a rarity, the plots of Regency novels contain very little violence, no sadism, no psychological perversions, no doom, no disgust; all turns on ingenuity, good humor, and surprise. It is the literary form of the minuet.

Explicit sex does not flutter the pages of a Regency novel. It is understood that offstage the gentlemen have their doxies, light-skirts, charmers, and the like. But the wise heroine, though aware of such peccadilloes in her suitor, turns a blind eye, and is, of course, herself chaste though spirited. Heroines occasionally elope, but seldom get very far. The worst escapade is likely to be the social sin of driving a high-perch phaeton down St. James's.

The great charm of the Regency period lies in the fact that it is just far enough removed from the present day to be picturesque, and yet not so far as to be uncouth. Our eighteenth-century ancestors' habits of diet and dress, their social manners and customs, were not too distant from our own; only far enough to make it interesting that they breakfasted at noon and dined at six, traveled by coach and took tea late in the evening. Lack of telephones and slowness of communication help with the ramifications of plot.

Still another attraction, I believe, is the fact that in this period, the middle classes had hardly made their appearance in fiction; Regency romances must necessarily be about the aristocracy, which in itself makes an irresistible appeal to the snob in the heart of every reader. Lord Orville, Fanny Burney's hero in *Evelina,* is the prototype Regency hero; though Jane Austen's heroes are not titled, they are all connected to aristocratic families; Mr. Darcy's aunt is Lady Catherine, Edmund's father is

Sir Thomas, Henry Tilney comes from Northanger Abbey. There is something quite fascinating about the *smallness* of London society at that time; there were only about 180 peers, and aristocratic society, the *ton,* consisted of about two thousand persons, who all more or less knew each other. When Caroline Lamb threatened Byron with a knife at a ball, the story was all over town in no time.

London must have been a charming city during the Regency period—elegant architectural crescents and terraces, their pale stucco unmarked, their symmetry unblemished; huge green parks and gardens surrounding lordly houses all buzzing with intellectual life. Fashion was changing rapidly. In a short period of time, the crinolines and powdered hair of 1775 shifted to the sylph-like Empire line of gowns of the early 1800's. At that time, a lady's whole toilette weighed no more than eight ounces; girls cropped their hair, damped their petticoats to make them cling, and wore silk shoes and satin mortarboards.

Although society persons were given to gambling, boxing, horseracing, dueling, and heavy drinking, they were also exceedingly well-educated; elegant, erudite, they studied conversation as an art form; gentlemen were judged by their graceful gait and deportment as well as their accents. A chapter in a book on polite manners was devoted to "How to take off your hat and replace it." One would have liked to live in that time; the next best thing is to try and depict it.

Who reads Regency romances? A wide, devoted, and growing market, judging by the regular reprints of the Georgette Heyer novels and her large school of followers. As the "straight" novel wanders farther and farther into offbeat realms, as limits of permissiveness in fictional violence and pornography become wider and wider, as suspense and detective novels lose ground and the market for Gothics becomes saturated, readers who need, from time to time, what might be defined as a safe, cheerful read, a nice book to curl up with in bed before going to sleep, must find themselves turning with relief to the Regency as one of the last sources of real escapist reading, pure, predictable, good-natured pleasure. The Regency is not one of your historic art forms; it is not going to open up new avenues or break down barricades or inaugurate cults. Its virtues are different. It is for fun.

I can remember an occasion twenty years ago when I had an elderly relative coming to stay with me for two weeks. She was in her late seventies, she was stone deaf, almost blind, she suffered from spasms, heartburn, nervous terrors, and a congenital feeling that she was being cheated, with a consequent surly suspicion of everybody's intentions toward her. I was not looking forward to the visit; I did not see how I was going to bear it. On my way to the station I stopped at a second-hand bookshop and happened to pick up a copy of Georgette Heyer's *Regency Buck*, which I had not read. Dipping into it, as I waited for the train, I could see that it was vintage Heyer. The sheer comfort that book gave me, reading a chapter every night during that exhausting visit, is something I still remember with warmth. If any Regency romance *I* write can give anybody such pleasure, however transitory, then I should feel that a complete justification for having taken to the form, which is all that any writer could ask.

11

THE ETHNIC ROMANCE

by Benyonne Lee

OVER $250 million worth of romantic novels sell annually to an estimated readership of twenty million. Is there any wonder that publishers are looking for new ideas for category romances in order to capture some of this tremendous paperback romance novel market?

One way to broaden the appeal of the category romance to contemporary readers without stepping out of very definite and preset story guidelines is to change the stereotype of the central characters. The passive, innocent, blond, blue-eyed heroine and the aggressive, wealthy, handsome, older, tall, dark hero of category romances do not meet the needs of a large segment of the romantic fiction readership today, nor do they typify the average reader—though the *average* reader is often looking for escape.

A new type of heroine is needed, one who would be typically American: high-spirited, independent, an individual woman whose life encompasses more than the traditional role of homemaker and childbearer (or secretary or nurse). She must be believable as a woman of the 1980s; one who can solve her own problems; one who is attempting to find a satisfying life. She need not be glamorous, but instead, intelligent, ambitious, and hard-working, usually in a career chosen through much thought. She must be a woman more like thousands of American women today and must reflect a more dynamic and flexible woman, no matter what her race or ethnic background.

The modern hero is different, too; he need not be too handsome, but still rugged and attractive. He need not have inherited wealth, or even be rich, but should be comfortably settled in a career he finds rewarding. Most of all, he must be sensitive to a woman's needs, gentle and tender or strong and assertive, as required. He must be aware of the modern conflicts between a man and a woman.

You must keep in mind that romantic fiction is fantasy entertainment. It should transport the reader into the realms of the exotic, whether in Tahiti or downtown Des Moines. Romantic fiction is escapist fiction that offers a satisfying short read costing only $1.50 to $1.75, even in today's inflationary economy. The reader of a contemporary category romance must be able to feel that she is the heroine in the novel, that she has the rewarding career, that she is being pursued by the relentless hero, and that he finally captures her with all his heart. The romance novel shows a side of life that is open to all men and women, no matter what their ethnic or racial background.

Ethnic stories have been around for years in the mass market field, for the reading public enjoys novels with exotic characters and settings. A recent issue of *The New York Times Book Review* showed that 67 out of 70 novels recommended for summer reading were ethnics: British, Spanish, Polish, Russian, South African, Indian, Jewish-American, or black-American. But not until the first black-American romance novel, *Entwined Destinies* (by Rosalind Welles, a pseudonym for Elsie Washington), was published a few years ago in Dell's Candlelight Romance line did ethnic characters appear as protagonists in category romances. These have included Chicanos, Cherokees, Mexican-Americans, Choctaws, and other minorities.

Interestingly, the new ethnic romance was not billed as being different from the standard contemporary romance featuring the typical white Anglo-Saxon Americans that dominate category romances.

What then is unique about these ethnic romances?

It is important to set the tone of the ethnic romance at the very beginning so that the reader knows beyond a shadow of a doubt that the characters are not the typical ones usually encountered in category romances. In my own novel, *Year of the Dragon,* the heroine is described immediately, in the first sentence:

> As the Star Ferry slipped out of its berth on Kowloon, Emily Eng edged near the railing to turn her dark, almost black almond-shaped eyes to the mainland of China.

Foreign settings are not unusual in contemporary category romances, but by the name alone—Emily Eng—the reader knows that the heroine is Chinese, which is unusual in these romances. Emily's ethnic characteristics are repeated throughout:

> . . . unnaturally tall for an Oriental . . . [which] set her apart
> from the other Chinese girls . . .
> . . . she hated to wear . . . the traditional cheong-sams, the
> long close-fitting Chinese dresses. . . .

The hero, of the same race and ethnic background as
the heroine, should be described similarly. In *Entwined
Destinies,* we see the hero thus:

> His skin was the color of burnished mahogany, and his
> head of close-cropped curly black hair was held high. . . .
> He was a replica of certain African chieftains who had
> visited her home when she was a child.

It is always easier for the reader to recognize the
ethnic background of the character from a typically
ethnic name (Luz Rivas, Mario Maldonado; Maria Su-
san Hawk, Dominic Cloud; Emily Eng, Richard Chu) or
from obvious physical traits. In another romance I am
in the process of writing, the heroine thinks:

> Sometimes, Flower had to concentrate very hard to think of
> herself as Chinese. For although she was born in China, she
> spoke English without a trace of the accent her mother still
> retained, and spoke Chinese only poorly. She was raised as
> an American, and thought of herself as such.

It is essential to portray the characters as being no
different in their thoughts or emotional reactions from
anyone else, though they may look different. The
heroine should have the same feelings of insecurity
when she meets the hero, the same antagonism towards
him, the same discovering love, as her blond, blue-eyed
counterparts.

An interesting setting (the *barrio* in Los Angeles; Paw-
huska, Oklahoma, the capital of the old Osage nation;
the British Colony of Hong Kong) can be used to distin-

guish the ethnic romance from its fellows, but it is not entirely necessary. In one sentence in her novel, *Web of Desire* (Dell's Candlelight Ecstasy), Jean Hager sets the location and the background of the heroine:

> This was Choctaw country, the place where her ancestors had lived since the early 1800's, the scene of her childhood and teen years.

And in *Desperate Longings* by Frances Flores (Dell's Candlelight Ecstasy), the heroine speaks of herself:

> I loved the *barrio* when I first saw it as a frightened, lonely ten-year-old arriving from Mexico. . . .

Since each of the above ethnic category romances was written by authors of the same ethnic background as the protagonists in their books, they were better able to avoid errors and unintentional racial slurs and could draw on sincere experiences. Rosalind Welles spent much time in Africa, and displays her extensive study of African and black-American history in *Entwined Destinies*. Marisa de Zavala, author of *Golden Fire, Silver Ice* (Dell's Candlelight Ecstasy), delves into her own up-bringing in a large Mexican-American family and describes a beautiful Mexican wedding ceremony in a Catholic Spanish mission. Jean Hager is part Cherokee and has used her knowledge of Cherokee mythology to advantage in *Portrait of Love* (Dell's Candlelight Romance), her novel about a Cherokee teacher.

Use of another language for an occasional phrase or word or sentence can enhance the ethnic romance. Here is an example from *Desperate Longings:*

> It was so natural for her at this point to speak to him in their own language. "*¿Tú sabes de que estoy hablando, verdad, Mario?*"

And from *Year of the Dragon:*

> Richard waved to the waiter standing by the kitchen door. *"Mai dan, m goi,"* he said sharply, and the check was presented to him.

Other little things, like distinctive foods, can be brought out by the writer to distinguish his or her book from the typical category romances. From *Yellow-Flower Moon,* by Jean Hager (Doubleday's Starlight Romance, a hardcover category romance line):

> . . . she found Josephine in the kitchen preparing ya-kah-pin, a traditional Osage soup made from the roots of water lilies.

In my novel-in-progress, I describe an intriguing Chinese dish:

> Called Buddha's Delight, it consisted of such exotic ingredients as ginkgo nuts, taro, tiger-lily buds, lotus roots, tree ears, and hair-seaweed.

The ethnic romance writer must be totally familiar with the culture and people about whom she or he is writing, in order to present an authentic picture. By making the setting exotic (Hong Kong) or ordinary (northeastern Oklahoma) or in-between (London), the writer can bring out the ethnic characteristics of the hero and heroine within the context of the story. And remember, the basic story in an ethnic romance is the same as in the other category romances; it always centers on the developing relationship between the hero and heroine.

The new ethnic romances have put a shot in the arm of the basically formula-type category romance novels put out by over eight publishing houses. Some editors are actively seeking ethnic romances, while others, though not discouraging, are not making any special effort to encourage writers to submit them. Some editors do not like the term "ethnic" and believe that the racial or ethnic backgrounds of the protagonists in a category romance should be secondary to the story. It is interesting to note that editors and publishers of young adult books are more receptive to ethnic stories than the more traditional editors of romantic fiction, who seem to prefer the tried and true for their older readers.

Basically, in writing the romance novel, ethnic or not, a writer must be aware of the five senses, for the romance novel is above all a celebration of the senses. It is not enough for the writer to describe the way a silk dress looks; the reader must be able to feel that silk dress (and in the case of the ethnic romance, the silk cheong-sam) on her body and hear it rustle as she walks. It is not enough to describe a kiss; the kiss (and in the more sensuous romances, the act of love itself) should be the culmination of a whole world of foreplay.

The ethnic romance has arrived and will be of increasing importance, because it expresses what a large segment of the reading public wants. And the reading public, as we all know, is not all white, Anglo-Saxon Protestant, but is comprised of a mixture of widely varied races and ethnic backgrounds. Members of racial and ethnic minorities have the same aspirations and desires as their white counterparts, and the dedication in *The Tender Meaning* by Lia Sanders (Dell's Ecstasy Romance), sums that up:

For Black Girls and Women (who need a dream)

Readers of these romance novels should be given

more realistic heroes and heroines with whom they can better identify. There *is* a greater need for category romances featuring various ethnic or racial groups, and readers should be made aware of the availability of these books when they are published and distributed.

12

WRITING TEEN ROMANCES

by Jane Claypool Miner

Pseudonym: Veronica Ladd

Imprints: Scholastic
First Love (Simon & Schuster)

TEEN-AGE romances are news right now. Girl-meets-boy stories have blossomed into big business, making the financial pages of *The New York Times* and *The Wall Street Journal*. After years of young adult novels featuring "heavy" problems, First Love (Simon & Schuster) and Sweet Dreams (Bantam) are selling like Wildfire (Scholastic).

Wildfire was the first, and I was there almost at the beginning. My Scholastic editor suggested I submit an outline for their new teen romance line. "They're just like your earlier books," she said. "Only keep the problems lightweight and put a little more emphasis on the romantic plot."

"How about cheerleading?" I asked. "Every young woman seems to have a love-hate relationship with cheerleading."

A few months later, my book, *Dreams Can Come True,* was published by Scholastic. It hit the teen best-seller list the first week and has been there ever since. (In the first eleven months it sold 250,000 copies.)

Teen-age romances are popular because readers identify with the characters and events in the novels. As a writer, I know my first job is to develop characters that young women can believe. If characterization is your specialty, you may want to try your luck at a teen romance. If you are a woman, know teen-agers, like to read love stories, and have a good memory, chances are that this is a natural market for you.

No matter how great your natural writing skill, you will find that writing teen romances isn't a snap. You have to walk a fine line between old-fashioned and modern, between romantic and wholesome, between realistic and exciting, and most of all, remain optimistic without sounding sappy. Reading even a small sampling of teen romances will convince you that they are often more sophisticated and realistic than their adult counterparts. Teen romances are not watered-down adult novels. Nor are they replays of old Faith Baldwin novels. They are a new and wonderful form of their own.

Once you have read several, you are ready to begin plotting and planning your own. If you are a published writer, an outline and partial manuscript (three to five chapters) may be acceptable to a publisher. If you are a beginner, you will need to submit the complete book (unless queries are specified in submission guidelines).

A successful romance combines character, plot, setting, and theme so tightly that the finished novel appears smooth and makes easy reading. I usually begin with a character who wants something. Recapturing that special adolescent emotion of yearning is a journey into my own past. Although my heroines' situations and personalities may be very different from mine, each of them experiences the same emotions I experienced as an adolescent. I was never even remotely interested in becoming a cheerleader, but I was extraordinarily interested in becoming a new person. In *Dreams Can Come True*, Elynne keeps notebooks of her hopes and aspirations as she tries to practice positive thinking. Like Elynne, I had great dreams, kept notebooks—and I still do.

I was never a Homecoming Queen as Karen was in *Promised Kiss*, but as a teen-ager I'd struggled hard with the question of conformity. These poignant adolescent moments of feeling apart from the group separated me from my group's values, just as Karen feels separate during her race for Homecoming Queen.

In *Senior Class*, Sandy, a black girl, is drawn directly from my personal experience. Like Sandy, I came from a poor family, and I had a great deal of ambition and direction. Like Sandy, I was a born go-getter and overachiever, and also like Sandy, life has taught me that gentleness and love are at least as important as achieving a goal.

Some writers fail because they do not identify with their characters. Perhaps they assume that in order to appeal to today's teen-agers, they have to write about "modern" young women who have it all together. Nothing could be farther from the truth. The young women in today's world have emotions and feelings very much like yours at their age. Their situations and circumstances may have changed, but their basic human needs have not.

To write a successful teen-age romance, one must

identify with basic human needs: the need to be loved, the need to be accepted; the need to be a leader in one's own group, the need to be oneself; the need to be successful. As teen-agers, every one of us has faced such questions as, how do I relate to the world around me? How do I find out who I really am? Teen-agers today are still asking for answers to those questions.

Each of my novels portrays a character who changes and grows. The problems in teen-age romances are everyday problems rather than unusual or tragic ones. During the 1970s, there were a large number of novels about teen-agers who were anorexic, obese, alcoholic, suicidal, and on and on. Some of the books were good, and some were bad, but eventually all of them blurred together into a dreadful gray parade of depression. They were no more realistic than teen-age romances, and they were a lot less fun to read. Whether Sandy will be able to go to college is a more realistic problem, and far more teen-agers are struggling with bad skin than with anorexia. Is it any wonder that teen-agers would rather read about whether Lisa will get a job or Elynne will get to be a cheerleader?

Each of my novels has what I call an external and an internal plot development. In *Promised Kiss,* the external plot has to do with Karen's Homecoming Queen contest, but the more subtle character-development plot (the one I think of as internal) has to do with how she feels about running for Queen and how important pleasing her mother and sister are to her. By the end of the book, she has learned enough about herself to accept the Queen's crown knowing that it is more important to her mother and sister than it is to her.

The plots are more than girl-meets-boy, girl-loses-boy, girl-finds-boy stories. They must be woven very carefully around the girl's ambitions and emotions.

The setting in a teen-age romance is very important. I try to select settings that are particularly visual and attractive. Cheerleading contests, homecoming games, flower shops, Cape Cod in the summertime, Olivera Street at Christmas are a few of my settings.

All of them would make lovely movies. The girls who are reading these books visualize the stories as they read, so the "prettier" the settings, the happier your readers are! Although settings should be realistic and detailed, long pages of description are not for the teenage reader. Teen-agers want to turn the pages quickly and get on with the story. Your readers will be much too intelligent to plough through pages of padded travelogue. Your setting should be so important that it is impossible to imagine the story happening anywhere else.

After you've found just the right characters, setting, plot, and theme, your work really begins. Remember that you're writing in a particular category—teen-age romance—and no matter how good your book is, if it doesn't fit the specifications, it won't sell. Your job is to deliver the right tone—wholesome, not sappy; sweet, not gooey. The tone is the magic, and it is magic that your readers pay their baby-sitting money for. They have expectations that must be met.

Your heroine must be a girl from fifteen to seventeen years old. Usually, she will come from a middle-class happy family. (I have chosen to write more than one story in which the girl had a divorced or widowed mother, but those are the exceptions.) The adults are secondary, and everything must be seen from the heroine's point of view.

The heroes are not the stylized macho characters of some of the adult romances; they are nice young men who remind you of the boy next door. If they are the kind of boys that will attract your heroine, they are the kind that her mother would approve of. Think wholesome and healthy.

Although the books are about relationships between boys and girls, they are not books about sex. The characters write love letters, hold hands, kiss, and might be permitted a fast squeeze or two, but there is no heavy petting and certainly no sexual intimacy.

The important thing to remember is that romance is sweet and young. Teen-age romances are about crushes, about relating to boys, and about emotions. They must be written with respect for a young person's feelings. The cardinal sin is for the writer to make fun of a girl's need to be loved and accepted.

Mine your memory for problems that seemed so important when you were a teen-ager: not being able to fix your hair like other girls; feeling fat; having acne; not being popular with boys. Whatever the problem, you must get inside the feelings of the adolescent reader facing similar problems.

I believe teen-age romances are so extraordinarily popular, not because they are frivolous, but because they deal honestly with wholesome values and emotions. I think girls are reading teen-age romances to learn how to handle their feelings and to help them sort out a set of standards and values that will serve them in today's world.

If you think love and acceptance are what make the world go round, maybe you should start writing your teen romance today. Begin with a girl who yearns for. . . .

13

FOLLOWING FOOTSTEPS IN THE HISTORICAL ROMANCE

by Rosalind Laker

Imprints: Doubleday
Signet (New American Library)

IT was my good fortune to be born into a family that took a great interest in its forbears. From an early age, I had tales handed down to me that fired my imagination and made the past seem real and alive, barely a breath away. When I became a writer, it was natural that in spite of writing many short stories and serials in contemporary settings that the historical romance should appeal to me most of all.

The great hurdle for all writers in this genre is to make the customs and social structures of the past appear natural to the reader. The scandal and disgrace that accompanied divorce and the total condemnation of the unmarried mother seem inconceivable to us nowadays, but to give authenticity to a story set in days gone by, it is essential to let the characters move within the framework of their own time, no matter how enlightened and advanced in their ideas they might be. Simply to put characters into costume and let them speak and behave exactly as they would today is to sacrifice atmosphere and plausibility. It is my experience that most readers like to learn from historical settings even when romance is the theme. Who could ever forget the Atlanta scene with the wounded or the subsequent burning of the city in *Gone With the Wind,* one of the best love stories ever written.

Another rule is never, never to skimp on research. If in doubt, check and check again. For my boxing scenes in *Warwyck's Woman,* for instance, I consulted the early 19th-century writings of Pierce Egan, who could be called the first sports reporter. When I had written my own bare-knuckle fight scenes, I asked a retired boxer to read them through for me, to be sure that no small error had slipped through.

Research is never a chore to me. When I have chosen a particular period in which to set my story, it is not enough for me to know the historical events of the time, but I must know what led up to them as well, in order to gain a fuller understanding. I read many topographical books dealing with the location, and whenever possible I visit the place. If this cannot be done, I study old photographs and visit national libraries where guidebooks of the period and other editions of the past give all the information needed. Old cookery and household management books are extremely useful for domestic backgrounds, dealing with everything from the treatment of those below stairs to the twenty-course dinners served at the master's table. As for clothes, the source lies in museums and in hundreds of good costume books, which means there is no excuse for putting an 18th-century heroine into *mink*, a fur completely unknown at the time. I always take into consideration the constricting effect of elaborate clothes. There was a time in the 1840s and 1850s when sleeves were cut to prevent a woman from putting up her arms to comb her hair or unbutton the back of her bodice, the emphasis being on feminine helplessness and dependence—a reflection on the male attitude towards her as a chattel. When large crinolines arrived, the gliding steps adopted by women were not affectation, but simply a necessity to prevent their voluminous skirts from swaying too much.

When my research is done and my synopsis prepared, I make two files. In one I put all the dates of the historical events, such as wars, political upheavals, etc., together with any other important incidents likely to have an effect on my characters' lives. I also include details and background of any historical personages who will enter into the story. In the second file, I list dates and events in the progression of the fictional story, enabling me to match fact and fiction as I go along. In this way, nothing slips out of sequence. A condensed biography accompanies each listed fictional character for quick reference if I should need it, because I know the ancestry and origins of each one of them, essential if they are to live and breathe out of the pages.

These are all the practical and methodical means by which I set about my writing. In addition, there is the sheer pleasure of walking paths that my characters, historical and fictional, have trod or are about to tread by way of my typewriter. Much of my inspiration has been drawn from my own family history. The Warwyck trilogy—*Warwyck's Woman, Claudine's Daughter,* and *Warwyck's Choice*—was based on the experiences of my own great-grandfather. His thirteenth child, born late in his life, was my grandmother, and thus in my own childhood, the best part of a hundred years was spanned for me in tales of his championship in the bare-knuckle boxing ring and his tempestuous career as a builder in a growing seaside resort. As I strolled the stretch of beach where Daniel Warwyck blasted out the rocks for his bathing-machines, his fictional shadow followed that of my great-grandfather, who had done the same on that very spot. The battle on the beach between Daniel and his workmen against the villainous element in the town was a repeat of another event that really happened. When in my novel poor Kate Warwyck grieved for the loss of two children from measles, and returned from their funeral to find that a third child had died, she was going through the suffering of my own great-grandmother. For *Smuggler's Bride* I was in my local district, where smuggling abounded in centuries gone by and a certain house known to me still has a smuggler's tunnel to the seashore. Moreover, to set my plot a-rolling, I had an eye-witness account of a smuggling incident handed down to me through three generations.

For *Banners of Silk* I went to Paris, seeking out the story of Charles Frederick Worth, the great couturier. He was the Englishman who taught the French how to dress. In 1845, at the age of twenty, he went to Paris almost penniless and with scarcely a word of French. Fifteen years later, he was designing dresses for Empress Eugenie and had become known worldwide. At Number 7, rue de la Paix, I looked up at the balcony where the initials *C. W.* still tell of the days when the rich and famous women of the day flocked to be gowned by Worth.

For another of my historical romances, I toured the great English country houses furnished by Thomas

Chippendale and heard the hands of the clock turn back to let me enter his life and his environs. I handled crystal scent bottles that he had fitted into the drawer of an exquisite dressing-table. I saw the green and gold lacquered furniture that is exactly where he placed it, the hand-painted Chinese wallpaper of his own choosing. I stood in the glow of the unusual lamps he designed, recently copied for a museum house in the United States, built in 1771. All these happenings are the gilt on the gingerbread of the writing I enjoy so much.

Readers often write to say that my characters are so "real." I appreciate the compliment, but see no cause for praise. How could I? In my own way I'm writing about characters, true and imaginary, who are always real to me. That is the grist of the writer's craft. I would not have it otherwise.

14

WRITING THE ROMANTIC SUSPENSE NOVEL

by Phyllis A. Whitney

Imprints: Doubleday
Fawcett Crest

THE type of novel I have been writing for many years has come under assorted headings. Gothic was a favorite label for a long time, though that word has a limiting connotation, and I wrote myself away from it. Recently I have been called a romance writer, though that's a name I reject because it doesn't include mystery. I prefer the label of romantic suspense, since this term comes closest to describing mystery-romance. Whatever they call our novels, there are many thousands of readers out there who enjoy this type of story, and if you like to write in this field, there should be a market for you. Certainly these books are being published under various labels.

When I start work on a romantic suspense novel, I like to think in terms of five preliminary headings. By "preliminary" I mean that period when I am searching for a direction, and before I get into serious plotting. These are the headings I like to use to keep myself on the track:

1. Setting
2. Heroine's vocation (or avocation)
3. Heroine's problem
4. Other characters
5. Mystery and romance

"Setting" is less obvious than you may think. It can be some exotic place you visit, or do extensive research about, or it can mean some more easily accessible spot in which *you* can create the right atmosphere. It's possible to imagine a fascinating house and the immediate area around set down in an ordinary and familiar background. I've done it both ways, and I know the important thing for me will be my own feeling about any setting. A good deal of the emotion in a story can grow from its background, so it must be one my own imagination can respond to.

When I first choose a place to write about, I have no idea what my story will be. The setting itself will help to trigger my creative juices, and the research is sure to be filled with story ideas as a new world opens up for me. Even when I'm making up the background wholecloth, research is important in stimulating the imagination. We need to put a lot of information in before anything comes out.

Some of this research may grow from the second listing: "Heroine's work or avocation." When I started writing adult novels I wrote only period stories. Then I began to be bored with the problems of my Victorian heroines, and for many years I've written about the present. I'm much more interested when my heroines have a foot in the world I live in, with all its complex and exciting problems. This means that each time I must find out what my main character does for a living. Today's women have an independence I admire, and I want the women in my books to fight their own battles. If you follow this course, make sure that your heroine's interests are ones you can sympathize with and understand.

I've stretched myself by writing about a woman who was a noted dress designer (when I can't thread a needle!). I got by with interesting research and by giving her a number of other matters to deal with. In my current writing I've been trying to give my main characters an interest in gardening—and it isn't going to work unless I can find an offshoot of the field that will interest *me*. A profession of any sort can lend color to a story and open up new plotting possibilities.

The next early matter I must decide about is a *personal* problem for my heroine. In the beginning there can be a division between her problem and the main problems that develop for her in the course of the story. In the end, both must come together and be resolved. In *Emerald* my heroine is fleeing across the desert to Palm Springs with her small son to escape a brutal husband. To save her son remains her main problem all through the novel. She has custody, but her husband means to kidnap the boy. Since child-snatching is a real concern today, this was especially interesting to handle.

However, the heroine's main problem should never stand still and become repetitive and tiresome. Other elements come in to affect it and develop future action.

In *Vermilion* my main character goes to Arizona to find out what lies behind her father's mysterious death. Such a search could quickly become boring if it doesn't grow and change. So other problems on the main road must emerge to keep the story moving and interesting.

My fourth heading, "Other characters," now becomes important. Working on the first three will suggest others who may populate your story. I try to think sketchily about these people and how they may help or hinder my heroine. I devise names for them, and identities begin to grow. Of course I make notes about every idea that comes to me, even before I do full character sketches.

I take time to think about my hero and the role he needs to play. Beware of the offstage hero who just steps in now and then. He needn't be in every scene, but he must play an active role in the story. Don't forget about him and leave him standing around for chapters at a time because you don't need him. It's necessary to figure out something for him to do. This isn't as obvious as it seems. There are a great many elements to juggle in any piece of fiction, and even heroes can be forgotten.

The emergence of the players in my drama brings me to the fifth listing: "Mystery and romance." Both difficult ingredients to handle well.

Every romantic suspense novel must have the element of mystery, since this is one of the best ways to build suspense. In any mystery curiosity should be strong at the start, and it's a fine tool to use in order to pull the reader along. We want our readers to ask, "What is happening here? What will happen next? Where are we heading?" Curiosity is a useful weapon, but it's never enough. Until our main character faces a goal she can reach only through tough obstacles, we haven't really begun our story. Yet a goal and its obstacles can't be established until a great deal has been made clear to the reader. So first we rely on curiosity. We explain through dialogue and action and move along, tantalizing, promising. When the real goal becomes evident, we're on our way. Though how we're to get there is what the story is all about. Mystery, of course, will continue right to the final scene.

This mystery and its solution seldom come to me in a single revealing flash. As the people in my story begin to flesh out and tell me about themselves, hints of mystery come to light a bit at a time. In the beginning I may have no idea of who the villain is, and I may try out several characters in this role before I can be sure, or decide what he's up to. Once he or she is settled, the mystery develops on firmer ground. The writer, at least, must know what's going on. We need to watch for surprise action—action that not only will astonish our readers, but will surprise us as well. For this reason I don't like to outline in great detail. I plan the direction of each chapter, and then I let my characters take over, so that they sometimes do things I never expected, and thus enrich my story.

Suspense is often a matter of pacing in the actual writing—and *rewriting*. Too much detail can kill a scene and slow down the pace, while not enough will make it lose color and interest. One develops a sixth sense about this rather elusive quality. In *Rainsong*, to be published in '84, there is what should be a suspenseful scene where my heroine finally corners someone who has been tormenting her with frightening tricks. In my first writing I tossed the scene away and spoiled the pacing. My heroine discovered at once that her intruder was "only a boy of sixteen." She was no longer frightened, and suspense went out the window. When I rewrote the scene, everything happens more quickly. A tall figure rushes toward her, nearly knocking her down. She doesn't recognize his youth, and the scene is much more frightening, the pacing is better (that is, the stretching out of suspense), so that when she meets the boy a few pages later and recognizes how young he is, she is still frightened. The young can be violent, and she knows he means her harm. We don't discover right away what he is up to, since it's necessary to build *more* mystery.

Of course once any puzzle is solved, we need to move toward the next surprise and a new rising of suspense. Pacing is important here as well. Too many exciting scenes too close together can weary a reader. So we rest the suspense for a little while, and build up gradually again. Always that rising and falling, but with a general mounting toward the heights of the climax scene.

Eventually, if you give yourself time to plan ahead, the mystery will be solved in that final dramatic scene that is a prerequisite for a suspense novel. By the time I come to the writing of the big scene, my imagination is sure to take over and give me answers that I may not have imagined ahead of time—perhaps better suspense than I could figure out with my "conscious" mind. That happened very nicely with *Emerald*. While I knew what my big surprise was going to be, I still didn't know exactly how I was to get rid of the heroine's brutal, child-snatching husband. Yet everything was there in the scene for me to use, and when the time came, my inner creativity took over and provided an original "weapon" for my heroine to wield.

Since we're talking about romantic suspense, we need to consider the romance itself. While the hero is always important, there may be some guesswork as to who really is the hero. Unsettling romances can be more interesting than those that are obvious from the first. If everything is right in the first scene, you have no story.

So you may want to keep the reader guessing here too. The scenes of emotion must, of course, be genuine so that the reader can feel with your heroine.

Whether or not it's necessary to write the torrid love scenes that editors seem to demand today, I'm not sure. In fact, there may be some shortsightedness operating here. Boredom can develop, and to write more and more "kinky" sex may not be the answer. From my mail I gather that a good many readers would prefer to see less explicit sex in the love scenes, and perhaps one of these days there'll be a stampede toward reticence as the pendulum swings. I still prefer to close bedroom doors on my characters, and I don't seem to lose readers on that account.

A last word. If you haven't discovered where you belong in all these "categories," you won't lose by experimenting. A certain amount of work for the wastebasket is part of most writers' learning process. Try—and if you fail, you'll still profit by the effort. Only by trying various forms of writing can any of us find our own niche. Romantic suspense requires a real stretching of the imagination, but if you can plunge into this make-believe world and make it absorbingly real for your reader, it can bring you success as a writer. Of course real satisfaction for any of us comes with mastery of our material and technique. That must always be our goal.

15

HOW (AND WHY) TO WRITE A ROMANCE QUERY LETTER

by Evelyn Grippo Bruyère
      West Coast Editorial Consultant
      Harlequin Books

SO you want to write a book? Well, why not? All other things being equal (like talent, the natural ability to tell a story, a half-way decent vocabulary and good grammar), you have as good a chance to sell as anyone else. But if you've never been published and plan to work without an agent, you must, and should, ask yourself, "How do I go about it?"

Surely anyone who's ever read a writer's manual or attended a writing class knows that the first thing you do when you have an idea, an outline, or a completed manuscript, is write a query letter to the publishing company to which you're planning to submit.

What is a query letter? It's exactly what the words imply. It's a letter that asks the publisher if he's interested in what you have written or plan to write.

A query letter (QL) is particularly important in the

107

case of the romance novel. With the proliferation of imprints flooding the market in the past year or so, and the profusion of titles within each imprint, the romance editor is inundated with submissions. Along the north wall of my office are floor-to-ceiling stacks of submissions: completed manuscripts, partials, hardcovers, and on one corner of my desk, a large pile of QLs.

With such a mass of material to work through, with so many covering letters to read, I'd be less than human (and so would any other editor) if I didn't read first the letters that catch my attention, that pique my curiosity, that otherwise intrigue me.

Eventually, of course, everything gets read—or at least skimmed. So why is it necessary to write this letter? Why not simply send in the material? Good questions. For one thing, from the author's point of view, it's a great time and money saver . . . providing you first do your homework. And what does *that* mean?

Homework: Let's say you've written a romance. It's a good story; your writing instructor told you so with great enthusiasm; your best friend, a romance buff, read it and loved it; and you know in your heart it's the best thing you've ever done. What do you do now? You do your homework. You go to your local public library and consult a copy of *The Literary Market Place* (referred to in the publishing community as LMP). This invaluable reference book contains information on every legitimate publishing company in the United States and, in many cases, around the world. Included in the publisher's listing is usually the name of the Editor-in-Chief (and, with many of the larger companies, the names of the editors in charge of the various categories, both fiction and nonfiction). Also included is a listing of the types of books, categories, and the number of books published per year by that publisher. *The Writer's Handbook,* also found in most libraries, includes the market requirements of major publishers looking for romance novels (and other categories as well), and *The Writer* Magazine, in its July issue and in its monthly Market News section, publishes the editorial requirements of publishing houses that bring out romances.

You will also find it useful to go to the two or three most active bookstores in your community and study the romance racks. Whose imprint is on most of the romances on the shelves? That's the company you should query first.

You now have learned three valuable pieces of information: 1) you know which company publishes romances; 2) you know the name of the editor who handles romances (or, failing that, you know the name of the editor-in-chief); 3) you know how many romances that publisher publishes (if the company only publishes two a year the chance of your making a breakthrough with that outfit is less likely than with a company that publishes six or eight or ten a year).

Why is it necessary to know the name of the editor? Because any of us would be less than human if we didn't gravitate to things that are directed to us by name. Ask yourself: If you got two pieces of mail at home, one addressed to "Occupant," the other addressed to you by name, and there were no identifying marks on either envelope, which would you open first?

What do you do now with the three valuable pieces of information? You sit yourself down and write the QL. And this is the hard part. How do you know what kind of query letter your particular editor-target likes? Many of us want a simple, uncluttered letter. Others want a more detailed letter. Then there are those of us who want to know something about you right from the start; others couldn't care less at that point, as long as the letter intrigues them.

The simplest way to handle it is to drop the editor a note and ask about the kind of query letter he or she prefers. Find out if there are company guidelines on how to submit material. If so, ask for a copy, and if a self-addressed stamped envelope is required, send your request off immediately. (Also, ask for other category guidelines if there are any available. You might want to switch from romance to mysteries or science fiction some day.)

Now you know what kind of query letter your editor wants. Let's say she or he wants a thumbnail description of the plot, a little biographical information, and an outline (synopsis) of the story. That sounds easy enough, doesn't it? There are, however, certain rules you can follow to make sure you catch, and hold, the editor's interest, to make sure she or he *wants* to read your outline, and ultimately, the material itself.

Let's try a sample letter.

Dear Mr. Jones:

I have written a contemporary romance that I think might be suitable for Harlequin's Superromances, set in an American colony in Rangoon, on the estate of a wealthy rubber plantation owner. The story concerns the courtship by the young American overseer, a man in his early thirties, of an American girl in her mid twenties. Each has been emotionally scarred by a previous love affair, and each finds himself/herself reluctantly falling in love, despite strong feelings of distrust of the other. Their romance is aided, abetted, and occasionally hindered, by the interaction of other members of the American colony there, and reaches a warm and happy conclusion despite the bitter-sweet memories of the earlier loves.

My husband was a plantation manager in Rangoon and we lived there for twenty years. I was active in local politics and am thoroughly familiar with the native customs and lore. My manuscript, titled *Rangoon Moon,* is approximately 75,000 words long, and is presently being retyped.

Attached is a synopsis of the plot. If this project interests you, I'll be happy to send you as much or as little as you'd like to see. I've also enclosed a stamped self-addressed envelope.

Sincerely yours,

As you'll see from the above, the letter gives a little of the plot, a little about the author, the present status of the material, and its length. Equally important, it lets the editor know that the author is familiar with the background of the story. Most important, it tells the editor instantly what category it's plotted for, an excellent time-saving device that works to the advantage of both editor and author.

The synopsis, incidentally, should include the beginning, the middle and the end of the story. There's nothing as frustrating to an editor as to get to the final paragraph, which should give the denouement, and read: "Major Rashid finally brings the lovers together, and how he does is the clever, ingenious climax of my exciting story." I want to know *now* how the story ends. There's enough paperwork for an editor from day to day without having to write an author to ask for a final paragraph so that he or she can decide whether or not to send for the entire manuscript.

Many authors include a synopsis in the body of the query letter. I personally have no objection to that . . . just so long as I know right off what the story's about. Neither do I object to the author including the first three or so chapters. (I always read everything that comes in, provided the query letter indicates that the material is in the areas I'm looking for.)

There's another aspect to the "why" of sending query letters—and an important one. I mentioned earlier that a QL is a great time and money saver, as indeed it is. Unless you don't care about money, it's a lot cheaper to send a query letter (twenty cents for the stamp, for either writer or publisher), than it is to send in a full manuscript, or even a partial, only to get a rejection if the material is unsuitable. Someone has to pay the postage for the return trip, and usually it's the writer. (I have an editor friend on the East Coast who told me that it's her company's policy not to return anything that doesn't include postage.) To sum up, if you're going to be rejected, it's cheaper—and faster—to get it on the basis of a query letter, self-addressed, stamped envelope included. And if you're going to get a nice, fat advance, you'll never miss those stamps.

All too frequently the writer, while carefully attaching a self-addressed stamped envelope, neglects to put her or his address on the letter itself. Much as we try to avoid it, occasionally an envelope will become detached from the letter (we carefully staple the envelope to the letter if there's no return address on the latter), and we're left with what might be a provocative query, with no idea of how to follow up on it.

Even if you decide to send in the complete manuscript, it should still include a query letter. Obviously, if I'm looking for adult romances and your covering letter tells me this is a juvenile, I'll return your material to you as soon as possible. If there's no hint as to its category in the covering letter, it might sit on a shelf for weeks before someone gets around to reading it, because as noted earlier, we're going to cover, as quickly as we can, the material we're actively looking for, and the only way we know that is from a query letter.

Another gimmick authors frequently use is to skip the query letter or outline and type the category on the title page (which, incidentally, should always include, along with the title and author's name, the author's (or agent's) address and telephone number (in case we're so excited about buying your book that we can't take the time to write!). Maybe we'll read that one a little sooner than the non-designated manuscript, but without knowing how it ends we'll return it if the first ten pages don't grab us. Had we had the details of the rest of the story, we might have continued reading, knowing that the beginning probably could have been fixed. After all, that's what an editor's for, isn't it?

Of course there *are* editors who don't want to be bothered with query letters or synopses; they prefer to read the first twenty or thirty pages, and if they're not hooked by that time, they'll reject it. But most editors want to know what the story's about. Even reading twenty or thirty pages takes time, and heaven knows most of us have little enough of that to spare.

One of the big hazards of sending in a QL is that a writer may say too little or too much, and then the editor may dump the project. Saying in your letter, "Enclosed is my romance novel titled *Rangoon Moon* which is 297 pages long. I hope you like it," obviously isn't enough. I can tell it's 297 pages long by looking at the last page (assuming you had the good sense not to paginate each chapter individually). But sending in a four-page letter which includes a brief synopsis and "Let me tell you a little something about myself. I'm the divorced mother of six children ages 5 to 28. My husband and I separated when the baby—named Joshua after my father, a Fundamentalist minister—was eleven months old. My oldest, named Barrington, my maiden name— was twenty-three at the time . . ." etc., is going to lose me by the time we get to the fourth child's name. That information may be important when and if the writer becomes a best-selling author, which, on the strength of that kind of letter, isn't very likely.

Writers *can* learn to create effective queries that will be likely to bring go-aheads from editors—especially now that the number of imprints in the romance novel field is proliferating, and the welcome mat is out to both new and experienced writers.

The Market

HARLEQUIN BOOKS

Harlequin Romances
Harlequin Presents

Jennifer Campbell, Senior Editor
Harlequin Books
225 Duncan Mill Road
Don Mills, Ontario
Canada M3B 3K9

What distinguishes a Harlequin? How can you prepare yourself to write a successful Harlequin? The best way is to read them—lots of them. Study the various authors' styles and approaches. Then let your imagination create a separate unique world—and take your reader into that world through your own distinctive narrative style. We at Harlequin believe our books are different because each author is encouraged to express this distinctive style. It is this freshness of approach and mark of individuality that we look for in new authors.

Harlequins are contemporary love stories—well plotted, tender and dramatic. They should evoke excitement, tension and a deep emotional and sensual response in the reader. To do this, you should develop your characters fully—make them believable and sympathetic. The heroine must be a woman characteristic of today's woman; background, circumstances, events and problems that shape her life should be realistic and modern. The hero should be a strong, dynamic character—assertive, even aggressive—but he can also be sensitive and aware. Remember that he, too, is falling in love, even though the heroine may not know it.

Conflicts in the developing relationship should be imaginative and unusual, and based on your characters' unique motivations and personalities. These conflicts should be strong counteracting forces that pose serious threats to the romance.

The sexual aspect of the romance should also reflect modern attitudes. Shared feelings and desires are central to the characters' sexual involvement, as is the heroine's deep emotional commitment to the hero. As in all aspects of plot progression, the sensual scenes should evolve naturally and convincingly, and be sufficiently long and descriptive to enable the reader to share the heroine's feelings. We are publishing a broad range of love stories, from the very gentle to the very sexy. Your criteria in this area should be what you feel most comfortable with, not what you think will sell your book.

Setting should be described with enough local color to convey a real sense of place. While exotic foreign settings are undoubtedly interesting, North American locales can be full of atmosphere and just as interesting to someone who has never seen them. Anywhere in the world is romantic to two people falling in love.

Above all, remember who your audience is and concentrate on developing the *romance* in your story.

Your manuscript should be 55,000 to 60,000 words, typewritten and double spaced on white bond paper. The original manuscript should be submitted; you should retain a copy. If you wish, you may send me the complete manuscript, but it is more economical to send the first fifty pages and a short synopsis.

*   *   *

Superromance

Star Helmer, Editorial Director
Harlequin Superromances
Worldwide Library
225 Duncan Mill Road
Don Mills, Ontario
Canada M3B 3K9

The overall objective of Superromance is to produce good solid reads with a contemporary tone (i.e., language, situations, characters and so forth), using romance as the major theme. To achieve this, emphasis should be placed on individual writing styles and unique ideas. (No previously published work will be reprinted as a Superromance.)

Heroine: Generally in her mid to late twenties, she should have a fairly clear idea of who she is as an *individual* and of her own self worth. Thus, due to her intelligence, maturity and gutsiness, she can certainly stand up for herself. If she does have a character flaw, it should be something she is aware of from the beginning of the story and learns to deal with in a constructive fashion. The Superromance heroine is most often from North America. If not, then the hero should be. She may be single, widowed or divorced. She should have a credible career about which the author can write with insight and authority. Lastly, the Superromance heroine is now ready to share her life and her love with the hero.

Hero: Handsome, passionate, self-assured, older than the heroine, he is a man who will ultimately be successful if he is not so already. While he doesn't have to be super macho, he must be a strong, sexy man, capable of tenderness, with his own needs and vulnerabilities. He can be single, widowed or divorced. He may be a North American or a foreigner. Never should he be physically abusive.

Plot: The story should revolve around multi-dimensional characters. It is told predominantly from the heroine's point of view, but the hero's perspective is welcome, too. The plot should be complex and imaginative enough to sustain reader interest, without forsaking realism. Ultimately a Superromance must be uplifting.

Subplots and secondary characters (preferably not children) *must* affect the major story line, but they should be interesting, emotionally moving or suspenseful in their own right.

The growing relationship between the hero and heroine should be based on more than pure physical attraction. Conflicts should have emotional depth, rather than result from convenient misunderstandings or superficial personality clashes. The realistic problems—and solutions—facing men and women today should be explored. Again, we are looking for a freshness of approach.

Locale: Either North American or foreign, the only criteria being that the setting is romantic and described in a natural way, rather than reading like a travelogue.

Style: Correct grammar and American spelling, except where improper usage is important to the depiction of the character. Please refer to the *Chicago Manual of Style* or *Webster's New Collegiate Dictionary* for detail questions.

Dialogue that is to the point, moves the plot forward, shades a character or develops the relationship is essential. Non-relevant information in either dialogue or narrative will be cut.

Sex: It may be explicit as long as it's written in good taste. Sex may be frequent, although it should never be gratuitous. The emphasis should be on shared sensual feeling. And don't forget the romantic aspects of relationships. Modern attitudes toward sex should be reflected while reinforcing the values of love, caring or commitment.

Summary: Superromances are 95,000 words long. The determining factor for publication will always be quality. Authors should strive to break free of stereotypes, clichés and worn plot devices to create strong believable stories with depth and emotional intensity. Superromances are intended to appeal to a wide range of romance readers.

A general familiarity with current romance fiction is advisable, to keep abreast of ever-changing trends and of overall scope. But we don't want imitations and we are open for *newness*—sincere, heartfelt writing based on true-to-life experiences and fantasies the reader can identify with.

The line is based on a mixture of new, as well as established authors. Contract terms are the same for both agented and non-agented authors.

Submission Procedure: For a new author—as complete a manuscript as possible, accompanied by a detailed synopsis of the balance.

For previously published authors—three chapters plus a long synopsis (approximately 20 pages), plus a copy of the author's most recently published book.

For authors the Superromance staff has worked with before—three chapters plus a lengthy synopsis.

*   *   *

American Romance

Vivian Stephens, Editorial Director
Harlequin's American Romance
919 Third Avenue, 15th Floor
New York, New York 10022

Harlequin's American Romances are contemporary stories of Attraction, Passion, Idealism and Love.

The American Romance line distinguishes itself from the traditional Harlequin Romances by featuring heroes and heroines who are American. The settings are in the United States and its territories and should give the reader a sense of place and culture that is uniquely American. (Just as the Harlequin Romances and Presents give the reader a sense of place and culture that is uniquely English and/or European.)

While the novels will contain some sex, the books will not be *overly* sexy or sensual and never carnal. The books are sensuous novels involving real people who confront the normal and often provocative problems of a modern relationship.

In general, the locale should be interesting with enough description to give the reader the feeling of being there. The hero and heroine should be mature adults with fully developed characters, engaged in the occupations and interests of today's world. The novels should be 70–75,000 words in length, and only *completed* manuscripts will be considered.

Heroine: She should be a mature American woman no younger than 26 years old. She *can* be older. She may have been married, widowed or divorced. If never legally married, her previous sexual experiences need not be discussed. She should typify the average middle-class American woman (the better for the reader to identify with). She need not be beautiful in the traditional sense of Anglo-Saxon beauty: tall, blond and willowy. The average American woman is not. But she can and should be physically attractive enough to appeal to the . . .

Hero: He should be a mature American male of any age compatible with that of the heroine. (That means younger than she or older or whatever.) He should be an achiever and upwardly mobile in his job. He does not have to own the company that he works for nor does he have to be rich. He should typify the average American male. He *does not* have to be tall, dark and handsome. He should be attractive in some way to appeal to and attract the heroine.

Setting: Must be within the United States. Characters may travel, and parts of the plot can take place in any part of the world provided that eighty percent of the novel takes place in the U.S.

Things to remember while writing an American Romance:

1.) Writing style should be of the highest quality, say that of a "best-seller."
2.) The viewpoint should be that of the heroine but the hero may also have a voice.
3.) The dialogue must be mature.
4.) The plot should be clearly defined and complex enough to keep the reader involved.
5.) Sex scenes should be fairly explicit without being graphic and *never carnal.*

Remember that you are writing a *romance.* A quality that should be sustained throughout the body of the work. Use your five senses to enhance the novel and look to your everyday life for ideas and inspirations.

❤❤❤

SILHOUETTE BOOKS

Contemporary Romance
Silhouette Special Edition
Silhouette Desire
Intimate Moments
First Love

Karen Solem, Editor-in-Chief
Silhouette Books
Simon & Schuster
1230 Avenue of the Americas
New York, New York 10020

Contemporary Romance

This guide is not a substitute for extensive reading of Silhouette Romances. To find out what a Silhouette Romance is, read as many as possible.

Though Silhouette Romances are always written in the third person, the point of view is almost exclusively the *Heroine's*. She is almost always a virgin, young (19–29), but not beautiful in the high fashion sense. She is basically an ingenue, and wears modest makeup and clothes. The book should open with an unexpected change, challenge, or adventure in her life which she accepts eagerly, although sometimes with trepidation. Her reaction to the amorous advances of the hero mirror the conflict between her desire for him and her strong belief in romantic love.

The hero is 8 to 12 years older than the heroine. He is self assured, masterful and hot tempered, passionate and tender. He is rich and successful in the vocation of his choice, or independently wealthy with some interest to which he devotes his time. Not necessarily handsome, but above all virile, he is never married to anyone but our heroine, though he may be widowed, and even divorced, providing it is made clear that the divorce was not his fault.

The Plot of a Contemporary Romance is built around the conflict between the heroine and hero; by the end of the novel this conflict is resolved and the lovers are together. The novel explores their developing relationship. We prefer their initial meeting, or the events leading up to their meeting, to be in the first chapter. Background material should be kept to a minimum of memories and flashbacks. After the lovers meet, the narrative should be sequential and straightforward. A Silhouette Romance is not a Gothic or a Novel of Suspense or Adventure. Murder, gunplay, abductions, beatings, spies, and the occult are not suitable elements for Silhouette Contemporary Romance.

Love scenes should be frequent and escalate in intensity. The lovers should not consummate their love without marriage. Descriptions of their lovemaking should be sensuous, not graphic. Rape and violence do not belong in a Silhouette Contemporary Romance.

The setting is always contemporary, preferably exotic or lush. Sense, taste, touch are all important. Dialogue should be natural. The writing, while contemporary, should not be slangy, obscene, or profane. Local idioms, dialect, foreign words and phrases should be used with extreme discretion.

We are asking for approximately 53,000 to 56,000 words, divided into no fewer than ten chapters and no more than twelve.

*   *   *

Silhouette Special Editions

Silhouette Special Editions are longer, more sophisticated romances, featuring realistic plots and well developed characters. As with the Silhouette Romances, these books are built around romantic tension.

The Heroine: A Special Edition is always written in the third person, but it is the heroine's point-of-view that shapes the novel. The heroine is generally 23 to 32 and she is intelligent and mature. Independent and accomplished, she supports herself successfully in her chosen profession and is never clinging or weepy. The heroine need not be a virgin. She accepts sex as a natural part of any loving relationship. She should be single when the book opens, but she may have been married in the past. If she is divorced, it must be clear that the divorce was not her fault.

The Hero: The hero, older than the heroine, is a dynamic, virile, supremely masculine man, one any woman could imagine herself falling in love with. Though he is self-confident, he also has a gentler, more vulnerable side, and may even admit to an occasional human weakness. He is never brutal or gratuitously cruel. Like the heroine, he may be a widower or divorced, but he is usually single when they meet. The narrative may sometimes include the hero's point-of-view in order to more fully develop his character and the plot.

Subsidiary Characters: Subsidiary characters never overshadow the hero and the heroine. They must be realistic, not stereotypical, and they often bring out aspects of the hero and heroine that aren't evident in their relationship with each other.

The Plot: In keeping with the sophistication of these books, the plots must be complex and believable. The plot centers on the developing relationship between the hero and heroine and the problems they must overcome on their way to a happy ending. The tension comes from a real problem that has to be solved and not merely from misunderstandings. This problem should be a realistic one, and deep enough to sustain the length of the book. It's crucial that the reader feel she is being presented with real people solving real problems, yet the story should never slip from the romantic to the mundane.

These books incorporate subplots that either complement the action or play against it in some way. The subplots, an integral part of the book, should hold the reader's attention without overwhelming the romance. Silhouette Special Editions are contemporary romances. Elements of mystery, suspense and the occult are inappropriate. These books are not Gothics, nurse-doctor romances or thrillers.

Love Scenes: The hero and heroine may enjoy premarital lovemaking, although the heroine should not be in any way promiscuous. The only man we see her go to bed with is the hero, and her feelings for him are always deep, even when she is unsure whether they are returned. The emphasis in the descriptions of their lovemaking is always on the sensuous and the emotional, not the graphically physical. The tone of the entire book should be romantic and sensuous, and this simply takes on increased importance in the love scenes.

Setting: American or foreign, the locale must always be interesting and appealing, an appropriate setting for romance.

Length: 75,000 to 80,000 words.

*   *   *

Silhouette Desire

The Heroine: The Desire heroine is a mature, capable woman of 25 to 32, who has a strong sense of her own individuality and an unshakable resolve to be happy no matter what obstacles she encounters. She need not be a virgin and is definitely not a naive young girl. Rather, she is a vulnerable, sensitive woman looking for a partner to share to the fullest the joys and challenges of life.

The Hero: The hero must be a realistic, believable modern man, one any woman could imagine herself falling in love with. He should be strong, caring, sexy and warm. He will tend to be in his mid to late thirties.

The Setting: Both international and American locales are encouraged, providing the setting is presented in a romantic and appealing way.

Writing Style: The writing should be extremely sensuous, providing vivid, evocative descriptions of lovemaking and concentrating on the characters' reactions to each other and the sexual tension between them.

The Plot: A Desire book centers on the developing relationship between the hero and heroine. The book should open with their meeting or the events leading up to it and end with their decision to make a lifetime commitment to one another. The tension and excitement in the book stem from the fact that neither protagonist is certain of the other's love until the end. Each scene must contribute to the process of discovery they're going through. The plot should not consist of a series of chance encounters, coincidences or filler scenes in which nothing substantial happens.

Emphasis: Desire books will emphasize innovative, unique plots, exploring realistic relationships that have been ignored up to now in other romance lines. They should depict the fears, doubts and problems, as well as the exhilarating wonder, of falling in love. Because Desire intends to mirror the real lives of modern women, marriages of convenience and similarly contrived situations are inappropriate for this line. For the same reason, realistic and detailed love scenes will be possible, providing they are tastefully handled. Sexual encounters—which may include nudity and lovemaking even when the protagonists are not married—should concentrate on the highly erotic sensations aroused by the hero's kisses and caresses rather than the mechanics of sex. A celebration of the physical pleasures of love, as well as its emotional side, should be an important part of these books.

Length: 55,000 to 65,000 words.

*   *   *

Intimate Moments

The Intimate Moments line is designed to appeal to readers looking for a heightened feeling of romance and fantasy in a category novel. The novel ought to sweep the reader away into a special world where everyday cares are forgotten in the thrill of passions that are frankly larger than life.

Heroine: The romantic heroine is the reader's entrée to the story. The events are seen primarily through her eyes, so it is essential that she be a sympathetic character. Independent, intelligent and strong-willed, she should also be emotionally vulnerable. Though she may find herself in circumstances unfamiliar to most readers, she reacts to them in a familiar and believable way. The reader should experience her fears and joys as though at first hand.

Hero: The hero is *not* the average boy next door. He should be a uniquely charismatic character, a man who has unusual presence and emotional strength. He may have overcome tremendous obstacles to rise to his present position; he has always lived life to the fullest. He feels at home in situations, professions and life styles which the average person rarely experiences. In short, he is the man every woman dreams about in her most exciting fantasies.

Setting: The setting may be foreign or American, but it should *seem* exotic and different. The story should introduce the reader to a new world. This may be accomplished by using a glamorous, high society background or an unusual locale, or by giving the hero and/or heroine offbeat jobs.

Love Scenes: The level of sensuality should be high throughout the story. Sexual tensions between hero and heroine will build until they actually make love—probably about halfway through the book. Several detailed love scenes—between the hero and the heroine only—should be included. There must be evidence of emotional commitment before they actually go to bed together.

Plot: The plot centers on the romance between hero and heroine, but it may incorporate elements of adventure, suspense or melodrama. These elements must never overshadow the romance; instead, they should be used to heighten the emotional highs and lows of the developing relationship between hero and heroine. The novel will be more action-oriented than the average romance, often dealing with life and death situations and always featuring an emotionally moving, dramatic climax. Ideally, it will elicit a few tears along the way, as well as a buoyant feeling when the reader learns that the two lovers will, indeed, live happily ever after.

Length: 75,000 to 85,000 words.

*   *   *

First Love

Silhouette's First Love romances are written primarily for girls 11 to 16 years old. For the most part, the story is told from the young heroine's point of view, although we do accept and welcome manuscripts from a boy's perspective. A First Love is particularly concerned with how a young girl handles her first relationship; however, these novels also explore common adolescent concerns such as peer pressure, shyness and the boundaries of parental guidance.

A First Love heroine is usually between 15 and 17, the hero is no more than a year or two older. The development of their romance is traced with sensuous, though not graphic detail. The tension of a First Love lies not only in the inevitable misunderstandings of a first romance, but also in the disparity between the heroine's romantic fantasies and reality, and her own desire to define herself as a person. In her attempts to win acceptance and recognition, the heroine often makes unexpected discoveries about herself and the world around her.

The style of a First Love, while colloquial, is standard English. We do not encourage heavy use of contemporary slang or dialect. These should be used sparingly and only when necessary for flavor or characterization. The tone of a First Love is upbeat, the ending optimistic. Values stressed are implicit and humanistic. First Loves are neither problem books nor moral tracts. Our aim is to give teenagers a good, light read that includes young characters, contemporary situations and universal themes.

We prefer to see complete manuscripts of 50,000 to 55,000 words, divided into no fewer than ten chapters and no more than twelve. We also accept a one- or two-page summary when accompanied by the first fifty pages of the novel.

*   *   *

Manuscripts for all Silhouette Books should be typed double-spaced, and the author's name, address, and telephone number should be included.

♥♥ ♥

DELL PUBLISHING COMPANY

Candlelight Ecstasy Romance

Anne Gisonny, Senior Editor
Dell Publishing Company
245 East 47th Street
New York, New York 10017

Ecstasy Romances must depict a compelling love story. The relationship must be realistically developed and bring into play all the channels of communication that are operating between two people in love. Yes, we want smoldering love scenes. But we also want to see our hero and heroine finding their way to each other through emotional and intellectual encounters as well. In other words, we want to see the emergence of a convincing, full-dimensioned and *mature* love affair.

Though the books certainly incorporate elements of romantic fantasy, it is fantasy grounded in reality. Ecstasy romances differ from the standard "sweet" romances, not only in terms of sensuous detail or extended love scenes, but in terms of characterization, motivation and plot. We are looking for warm appealing characters that have been rendered with insight and texture; characters that a reader will care about.

Though we have no rigid guidelines regarding the placement and content of love scenes, we do feel that sexual chemistry and emotional involvement do bring men and women together in the most wonderful ways. Sensuous, non-explicit presentation of this side of a love affair should be part of an Ecstasy Romance. But whether the encounter is a quick kiss on her fingertips, or a night of passion, the scene is always one of idealized love; the emphasis is on a seduction of the senses (taste, smell, touch) and an intense, convincing emotional exchange between the protagonists.

Though there are no hard and fast rules for our line in regard to plot, characterization, etc., there are a few things to keep in mind if you're submitting a manuscript for our consideration.

Most Ecstasy heroines are between the ages of 25 and 35; most are established in an interesting career. Avoid the use of formula plot devices such as a marriage of convenience between the protagonists, or amnesia. These romances are essentially sensuous, realistic contemporary stories *set in the United States*. We prefer that writers focus on developing the relationship between the hero and heroine and that conflicts in the story arise out of this relationship (i.e.: career vs. marriage, unresolved feelings regarding a prior relationship, etc.).

Love scenes should be tastefully handled without being pornographic, or overly explicit.

We will consider completed manuscripts of 50,000 to 60,000 words (approximately 200 to 225 typewritten, double-spaced pages) or partials of 50 to 70 pages in length, containing a detailed synopsis and outline.

BERKLEY/JOVE PUBLISHING GROUP

Second Chance at Love
To Have and To Hold

Ellen Edwards, Senior Editor
The Berkley/Jove Publishing Group
200 Madison Avenue
New York, New York 10016

Second Chance at Love

Second Chance at Love books are light, escapist, contemporary novels, 60,000 words long. The love story between the hero and heroine—who is getting her second chance at love—is always in the forefront of the action of the novel. The story is told in the third person from the heroine's point-of-view.

Category romance has grown a lot in the last few years and the reader has a much wider variety of romance lines from which to choose. It is therefore increasingly important that you make your book stand out by including fresh and original elements, creative plot twists, and unusual situations. Creativity combined with the beloved traditional elements is absolutely necessary.

Plot: The plot is the love story of the heroine and the man who is her "second chance at love." Her first relationship must have been serious enough for her to have felt she was in love and committed, and it must have ended before the start of the novel. The heroine can be a divorcée, a widow, or perhaps jilted for a reason that does not reflect badly on her. Or she may have become disillusioned about men and be devoted to her career, or have had family responsibilities. These are, of course, only some of the possibilities—creative twists are welcome.

The hero, "Mr. Right" (the second love), is introduced in the first chapter—in fact the closer to page one, the better! *The new romance* is the subject of the book, but the heroine's background has to be

included in the story. Despite the conflicts and complications between the heroine and hero, the story is upbeat in tone. A light touch
is all-important in the treatment, since these novels provide readers
with an escape from their real-life dilemmas. Therefore, controversial social issues (nuclear power, right to life, etc.) and serious personal problems (alcoholism, mental illness) are to be avoided. Elements of suspense/intrigue and gothic touches are not permitted—
for example, there are no kidnapping, blackmail, or murder
schemes in Second Chance at Love novels. We're always looking for
work that is witty, as well as very sensual and romantic. Humorous
situations and clever dialogue require skillful handling, but can help
maintain a light tone and make the story very entertaining.

In brief, then, a Second Chance at Love author must create a
heartwarming and exciting love story. The writer's job is to get the
heroine and hero together, keep them together, make sparks fly, put
obstacles in the path of true love, and finally resolve the complications and the story on a high note with a satisfying ending.

The Heroine: Aged 26–40, and an American, the heroine is not
naïve and virginal, but rather a mature young woman who has already had a serious love relationship. (This first relationship has
ended before the start of the novel.) She should be attractive, appealing, and spirited, yet a vulnerable person the reader can admire
or like, and cheer for—in short, a woman the reader really cares
about. Although the failure or loss of her first love has made her
suffer, she must never be portrayed as depressed (or depressive!).
Even in the beginning of the story, she has a vivacious personality.
She should have either a profession, a great interest (sports, the arts,
etc.), or a demanding job in or out of business. She should not be a
typing-pool level secretary, but executive/administrative assistant
positions are definitely acceptable—she may be an aide for the top
executive she falls in love with, or she may replace someone else on
an important assignment. If she does not work, she must have a
serious interest that shows her to be a well-rounded person. Such a
career or interest helps to provide plot elements. Often it is the
means through which the heroine meets the hero, or the reason she
is in the place where the novel is set. The Second Chance at Love
heroine rarely crumbles in a confrontation, blushes, cries, or runs
away. She does not tell outright lies, although she may hedge in
order to spare someone's feelings.

The Hero: The hero is virile, masterful, and attractive, though not
necessarily handsome in the conventional sense. He is tender and
sensitive. He is generally not more than five to eight years older than
the heroine, from late twenties to mid forties. He can be American

or foreign, and while he need not be rich, he must be successful. He can possess a complex personality, but serious problems such as alcoholism, impotence, addictive gambling must be avoided. He need not be "brooding," the "strong, silent type," or any of the other stereotypes found in traditional romances. He may be open, honest and amusing. In short, he should be the kind of man *you* would want to fall in love with. In addition, there cannot be "gothic" elements associated with him. By the end of the book, the reader should be sure that, with her second chance, the heroine is getting Mr. Right. However, the hero can be the same man the heroine was previously in love with, especially if they parted through a misunderstanding or circumstances beyond their control.

Other Characters: The brutal, sophisticated "other woman" is an overused device. If you include the "other woman" (and she is not a requirement), make her as original as possible. She need not be a villain; we prefer that she be a realistic character with both good and bad characteristics. If you include the "other man" (and, again, he is not a requirement), make sure that he does not reflect badly on the heroine by being someone who is so unlikeable that the heroine should never have gotten involved with him in the first place.

Children: The hero and/or heroine can certainly be parents, and children can play an important role in the story. But they should never interfere with the hero and heroine's lovemaking and, to insure this, they *may* need to be sent offstage temporarily. In addition, children should not be the main source of conflict between the hero and heroine. Again, there should be no gothic elements: the heroine should not be hired to look after the hero's children. Broken homes are often the rule rather than the exception in today's world, and we welcome fresh and tasteful treatments related to this contemporary problem.

Setting: The setting should add to the romantic atmosphere, enhancing the love story. It can be either within the United States or abroad.

These novels take place in the "everlasting present," which means that no specific reference can be made to a particular event in history. For example, our couple cannot have been separated by an event as specific as the Vietnam War, since such a reference would indicate that they were separated no later than the early 1970s. The reader must always feel that the story is taking place right now as she reads it.

Sex: The hero and heroine do make love even when unmarried, and with plenty of sensuous description. No clinical terms ever! Orgasm and excitement must be described in somewhat poetic (metaphorical) language. The setting and circumstances of the love-making are also crucial, and should contribute to a build-up of sexual tension.

It is important to note that, even though the couple make love while unmarried, there is no adultery—both hero and heroine, if previously married to people still living, are definitely *divorced,* not just separated or even waiting to sign divorce papers, before they make love.

Most vital, however, is that a strong emotion (anger/embarass-ment/sympathy/physical attraction) must exist between the hero and heroine from their first meeting. Sexual attraction to the hero must be recognized early on and should be drawn out to maximum effect. The interest lies in the physical awareness, sexual tension, conflict, and growing love between the two main characters. The heroine's physical responses to the hero should be described often throughout the story.

Mild lovemaking should be introduced as early in the story as is convincingly possible and should gradually build in intensity until the couple actually makes love, by about halfway through the story. They should make love at least once more in the second half of the book. Actual lovemaking should be described in considerable length—in several pages rather than in several paragraphs—and with plenty of sensual detail.

Point-of-View: The story should be told in the third person *from the heroine's point-of-view.* The reader knows only what the heroine knows. Action that goes on when the heroine is not present, or thoughts and impressions held by other characters but not directly communicated to her, do not appear in the text. However, the fact that the story is told through the heroine's point of view does not mean that the hero's attitudes and feelings are not known. They *are* revealed through the dialogue and action.

Third-person, heroine's point-of-view is difficult for some writers to understand. It's like the first person. Only what the heroine sees, feels, hears, thinks, guesses, and so forth is allowed. Jumping into another character's mind is not allowed. Describing something through the eyes of another character or from an all-knowing point-of-view is not allowed.

Second Chance at Love editors believe it is this technique which in large measure helps to insure reader identification with the heroine and keeps tension building with that all-important edge of doubt and insecurity (He loves me. . . . He loves me not!). Of course the reader knows something the heroine doesn't—that the hero loves her madly—but the device still works. It helps to recreate for the reader the thrilling anxiety everyone experiences during the phenomenon of "falling in love"—and that is what these books are all about!

Description: Vivid detail and poignant observation do not merely enhance the story—they are vital to it. The heroine and hero should be physically described when they first appear, and descriptive touches should be worked in throughout the novel. Clothing (the heroine's particularly), food, decor, scents, colors, unusual aspects of the setting should be handled deftly. A few carefully chosen observations make person, place, or thing real and exciting for the reader, while excessive description—a listing or cataloguing—does not. Select and prune, and as you do, remember to focus on the sensual.

Other: Use lots of dialogue and make it as lively, snappy, gripping as you can. Action—which includes good dialogue—leads to excellent characterizations. Demonstrate. Don't explain in long narrative and don't "tell about" a person or episode. Show the reader. It makes writing spring to life.

Limit severely the use of flashback. No flashforward, please, but a couple of sentences in the novel foreshadowing an event or emotion may be included.

The following list contains devices that we feel have been sadly overworked and should be avoided:

1.) The heroine is too often a journalist, photojournalist, artist, writer, archaeologist, travel agent, or is connected with a resort or hotel.
2.) The hero is too often an architect, archaeologist, artist, photographer, travel agent or is connected with a resort or hotel.
3.) "In-motion" scenes (i.e., a scene with the heroine in transit—by boat, plane, car, bus or train—to where the main action of the story will take place) are overused as openings in the manuscripts we see.
4.) The following settings have been overused: Mexico, Italy, Greece, and the American Southwest (Arizona, New Mexico, Texas and any desert or dude ranch).

How to Submit Manuscripts: Submissions are welcome from both agented and/or published writers as well as from unagented and/or novice writers. Manuscripts must be neatly typed, double-spaced, with at least one-inch margins on both the right and left sides of each page. Use standard-sized white bond paper.

Published writers may submit either a full-length manuscript or a proposal consisting of a complete synopsis and several sample chapters of the work. If possible, we would like to see a copy of a previously published work; if not, a brief outline of your publishing history. Unpublished authors should submit a complete manuscript. If you have doubts about the suitability of your work for our line, please send a query letter before making a submission.

No simultaneous submissions please! We respond to submissions with all due haste. Also, we will send an acknowledgment upon receipt of your material.

Please enclose a stamped, self-addressed envelope or mailer with your submission.

Be sure to keep a copy of any material you submit.

Study the guidelines carefully and read Second Chance at Love romances as they become available to make sure that the manuscripts you submit meet the editorial requirements for this line.

*   *   *

To Have and To Hold

To Have and To Hold books are contemporary romances distinguished by their theme: marriage. In these innovative, 60,000-word books, a married couple faces a problem or conflict and resolves it happily, ending with a deeper commitment to each other. These romances do not belabor the mundane details of married life, nor are they case studies of how to save a failing marriage. Instead, they are warmhearted, compelling love stories depicting marriage as fun, adventurous, enriching, exciting, sometimes problematical, and above all, romantic. They are peopled by well-developed characters with mature attitudes, and they revolve around convincing conflicts and believable situations.

Marriage, a complex and multi-faceted relationship, often involves ups and downs, hard times, moments of doubt and dissatisfaction. In To Have and To Hold romances our heroine and hero will work through a specific problem or a related series of problems and will grow individually and together in the process, achieving a deeper, more meaningful relationship and a better understanding of themselves and each other. Writing about a married couple allows you to explore creatively a wide range of attitudes and conflicts. Still, it's essential to maintain a light, sensitive touch, since these novels provide readers with an escape from their real-life dilemmas. The conflict should never be so serious, heartbreaking, or controversial that it detracts from the entertaining nature of the romance. Humorous situations and clever dialogue require skillful handling, but we encourage you to try them.

In brief, then, To Have and To Hold romances affirm that love, romance, and good times can and do exist within marriage; that in marriage two dynamic partners can find closeness, stability, security, sharing; that they can rely on each other during difficult periods; that they can grow, change, and achieve a better life.

There are few literary precedents for this concept. We're breaking new ground. And we're asking you to call upon your imagination and ingenuity to create a truly original contribution to the world of romantic fiction. Remember, history, the arts, media, and the people around you provide many prototypes. Think of cinema's sophisticated handling of a couple's personal vs. professional goals in the Tracy/Hepburn classic, *Adam's Rib;* think of the romantic camaraderie (*not* the occupations) of television's celebrated twosome, *Hart To Hart;* think about a marriage between a contemporary Scarlett O'Hara and Rhett Butler (or any of your other favorite romantic heroines and heros) if *Gone With The Wind* had ended "happily ever after." Don't try to duplicate any of these examples in your book—just consider the endless possibilities and let your creative juices flow.

Heroine and Hero: They can be any age (26 to 40 is most successful in our experience), and their existing marriage can be of any duration. They are attractive, appealing, motivated people the reader will really care about. Of equal importance, they are responsible adults who are committed to their marriage, despite the problems they face. They are fully-developed characters with convincing strengths and weaknesses.

Secondary Characters: Their presence contributes to the developing relationship between the heroine and hero. They are realistic, interesting people—not stereotypes—and should be as fully developed as possible given the length of the books. If you choose to use another woman or man as the basis of the conflict between the hero and heroine, be sure to avoid the stereotypes that are too often relied on in category romances (i.e., she's a brittle, sophisticated *femme fatale;* he's a nice guy, but dull). We're looking for fresh, original secondary characters who contribute to the story in unique ways. If you choose to include children, be sure they, too, are realistically drawn and interwoven throughout the story.

Sex/Lovemaking: To Have and To Hold romances are sensuous love stories, and the heroine and hero should make love several times. Actual lovemaking should be described in considerable length—several pages rather than several paragraphs—with plenty of sensual (but not clinical) detail. We encourage fresh approaches to lovemaking. Sex can be playful and fun as well as intensely passionate. The couple can make love in many different settings, under many different circumstances. The most important element here is emotion—what the characters are feeling. The mood can be affectionate, intimate, passionate, angry, comforting, etc. The lovemaking scenes should never be gratuitous; rather, they enrich the story by bringing about new developments in the heroine and hero's relationship, or by reflecting changes that have already occurred.

We prefer that you *not* use a marriage of convenience. Such a device is not convincing in a contemporary romance.

Please Note: Adultery (sex with someone other than the spouse) is *not* acceptable. The heroine and hero may be tempted to make love with another person, and can even seriously consider it, but they should never break their marriage vows.

Violence of any kind (including rape, child abuse, wife beating) is also *not* acceptable.

Point of View: The story can be told in one of two ways:
1.) in the third person from the heroine's point of view
2.) in the third person from both the heroine and hero's point of view. (But if one voice predominates, it should be the heroine's.)

Note: Be careful *not* to slip into other characters' points of view, or to tell the story from an omniscient (all-knowing) point of view.

Setting: Many readers express a preference for American settings, and many so-called glamorous locales have been sorely overused. Use your discretion, but remember that descriptions of the setting (including clothes, food, people, places and things, etc.) help tremendously to enrich a story; set a romantic tone; allow the reader to learn, travel, and live vicariously. We welcome unusual settings or new approaches to well-known ones. But be sure you know the locale well or have researched it thoroughly.

Manuscript submission: Follow the guidelines for Second Chance at Love.

♥♥♥

NEW AMERICAN LIBRARY

Rapture Romance

Robin Grunder, Editor
New American Library
1633 Broadway
New York, New York 10019

Readers look for a number of things in a romance novel: an interesting plot, sympathetic characters, a strong love story, and a happy ending. They want a book they can relax with, one that will provide them with a pleasant fantasy into which they can escape and will leave them with a satisfied feeling at the end. In a romance, if nowhere else, everything works out for the best in the best of all possible worlds.

At New American Library, we have worked to make the distinguishing characteristic of each novel in our Rapture Romance series the creation of an imaginary world that reflects the real world, but enhances the emotional drama of a passionate love affair.

These medium-length (55,000 words) contemporary romances are aimed at the reader who wants more romance, more passion, more sensuous and sensual detail than is found in traditional romances. They feature provocative situations that explore any of the possibilities that exist when today's men and women fall in love. The heroine and hero become intimately and intensely involved early in the plot and make love several times throughout the course of the romance, and each passionate kiss, each tender caress, each earthshattering climax is described at length, in lavish, specific (though not clinical) detail. The plots are sophisticated and modern, but they must remain wonderful fantasies with no grim or tragic elements and no elements of mystery or suspense.

Rapture Romance novels are not written down to their audiences. We know that romance readers demand a skillfully worked plot, fully rounded characters, and evocative descriptions, and we look for writers who are not only good story tellers, but who can turn a nice phrase or set down a telling detail. Of course, though there's more emphasis on, and therefore space taken up by, the physical expression of the hero's and heroine's love and desire, the most important element is still the love story. The relationship must develop in a believable way, proceeding logically from first encounter to first kiss to lovemaking: we do not expect the hero and heroine to jump into bed the minute they meet, and careful thought should be devoted to setting up a situation in which rapid intimacy is plausible.

The plot of a Rapture Romance should be believable in terms of today's lifestyles, and we expect the problems that come between the hero and heroine to be the kind that occur between adults with well-defined opinions, ambitions and morals, and the misunderstandings to have supporting evidence that couldn't be set aside simply by asking the loved one a few questions. And when all conflicts are resolved, the solution arrived at will be an equal compromise, or a change of mind based on new information—for example, the discovery of true love would make a hero who doesn't want to be tied down propose, most likely to a heroine who can accompany him on his expeditions into uncharted jungles. Needless to say, although the heroine and hero may or may not continue to make love while misunderstandings and conflicts remain unresolved, when they are ready to admit that they love one another, and believe in each other's love, they will agree to marry (or if separated, renew their vows).

We feel that the old-fashioned, stereotyped characters—the simpering, submissive heroine, the brutal and violence-prone hero—are no longer interesting to readers who are ready for more sophisticated fare. The heroine of a Rapture Romance is youthful, but she has a sense of maturity that manifests itself in her dedication. She's attractive, but not necessarily ravishing, and she does not dwell despairingly on her looks. If she is indeed ravishing, she knows it and enjoys it as she would any other natural gift, and if merely attractive, takes pride in her good points (thick, shiny hair, fit and athletic body), and makes the most of herself, then forgets her appearance—other things are more important. She is capable and resourceful, but never strident and domineering, and could conceivably be shy or of a quiet nature. She is not a timid, shrinking violet or bumbler who has to be rescued constantly, although the hero can smooth over a rough moment for her, as the heroine will do for him. We wouldn't, for instance, be surprised to see the heroine's knowledge of first aid used to help the hero when he sprains an ankle. However, she may at times be overconfident, and certainly she should be able to laugh at herself or admit to a mistake. Finally, it is important that the heroine not be simply a passive object of the hero's attentions or the plot's twists, but contribute actively to the plot's development. The heroine is always American.

The hero is older, not necessarily fabulously wealthy, but successful at what he does. He is attractive in a masculine way with an athletic but not muscle-bound build. Although strong-willed and determined, he is not a bully and can, when necessary, be gentle and supportive. He not only loves the heroine for her beauty and desirability, but respects her abilities. In fact, he comes to realize that he would be unhappy with a weaker, less accomplished woman. This

respect may come grudgingly. The hero may or may not be American.

Since the emphasis in Rapture Romance is placed heavily on the
physical expression of love, it is important that each love scene (and a
love scene can be something as simple as the look two people exchange, the unexpected electricity that flares between strangers, a
quiet moment of unspoken sharing) be an integral part of the plot
development and contribute something new to the relationship, that
it have its own mood. Foreplay and afterplay, with descriptions of
what the heroine thinks and feels, what the hero says and does,
before, during and after making love can provide this, as can a
change in setting (i.e., outside in the afternoon rather than in the
bedroom at night); a switch in the seducer/seducee roles; a change
in the level of experience or attitude of one of the participants; an
infinite number of distinctions can be made. And the love scenes
should be described in full and lavish, though not clinical, moment-
by-moment detail. We don't want to know that he is handsome, we
want to know that he has crisply curling black hair with just a touch
of gray at the temples. We don't want to know that the moonlit night
was romantic, we want to know that the sky was a dark velvet canopy
over their heads, and as they walked barefoot at the edge of the
ocean the cool water tickled their bare feet and the rush and roar of
the ocean seemed to echo their own heartbeats. We don't want to
know that his touch aroused her, we want to know that the rough
feel of his calloused fingertips as he wonderingly explored the outline of her face with feather-like caresses set her trembling as no
arrogant and inescapable embrace could have. It is important that
the reader at all times feel the strong mutual desire of the hero and
heroine, their constant awareness of, and fascination with, each
other.

Of course, physical attraction is not the only thing that brings the
heroine and hero together. We should see, not be told about, the
reasons that these two people are unique, and uniquely suited to one
another—in short, they not merely desire, but love each other.
There should be little if any reliance on alcohol as a reducer of
inhibitions—though we have seen emotional crises which worked
well for that purpose—and *no* rape or coercion. These are normal,
healthy adults who love each other and know what they want. When
appropriate, their relationship may also include a sense of fun—
gentle teasing, mock wrestling matches, etc. However, this does not
preclude the darker side of passion, as long as it does not become
abusive.

Finally, the important thing to keep in mind about writing a Rapture Romance is that you should enjoy creating it. Write about things

you know, things that interest you, things you find romantic, and men you could fall in love with. The little details will make the story rich and more real than any formula story. Do not try to copy other people's plots or characters, but, while keeping in mind our general rules, make your story unique. If the characters live in your imagination, and the story touches you, your sincerity will show, to an overworked editor or a reader bombarded with choices!

BANTAM BOOKS

Loveswept

Carolyn Nichols, Senior Editor
Bantam Books, Inc.
666 Fifth Avenue
New York, New York 10103

Loveswept romances feature true romance, sensuality, and touching emotion. The first chapter must be especially riveting, starting the story on a high plane of involvement and building higher and higher with each succeeding chapter. The relationship between the hero and heroine must develop in a believable way and focus on producing real emotions in the reader—laughter as well as tears. The heroines and heros range in age from 18 to 45. The heroine may be young and naive, but never stupid. At any age she must be bright and independent; the hero is strong, yet sensitive and appealing. Loveswept novels are quite sensuous and sensually detailed. Tired, overused devices such as the marriage of convenience, wimpy men and bitchy "other" women should be avoided.

We publish only three 55,000- to 60,000-word romances each month. And, while we consider carefully each submission (even those of unpublished authors), we are very selective. We think more in terms of developing an author than "buying" a single work. Loveswept might be called "the author's line." The inside front and back covers of our novels feature a photo of the author along with her autobiographical sketch. Pseudonyms aren't used.

SCHOLASTIC PUBLISHING, INC.

Wildfire
Windswept

Ann Reit, Editor
Scholastic Publishing, Inc.
730 Broadway
New York, New York 10003

Wildfire and Windswept are for girls aged 12 to 15. Manuscripts should be in the 40,000- to 45,000-word range, have good character delineation and plot development, and include no sexual involvement between hero and heroine, except kissing and feelings of attraction. The theme of each line is different, however.

Wildfire: Plots deal with realistic problems of young girls in first or early relationships. Heroine is 15 or 16, hero 17 or 18.

Windswept: Contemporary gothic romances about real girls who become involved in the "gothic" situation through realistic events. The first chapter should carefully develop who the heroine is, so the reader identifies with a *real* teen-age girl. The mystery should develop along one strong plot line in contrast to the old-fashioned gothics, which have numerous sub-plots. Equally important to the mystery element is a strong romance between the 16- or 17-year-old heroine and the hero, who is 18 to 20. There should be no occult elements in Windswept books.

BALLANTINE BOOKS

Love & Life

Pamela Dean Strickler, Senior Editor
Ballantine Books
201 East 50th Street
New York, New York 10022

Ballantine is looking for very high quality, contemporary novels by and about American women in the 1980s for our Love & Life list. Each should be a unique story—about people and situations that are true to life. While romance is an important element in these novels, it is not the dominant theme. What we want is psychological realism in women's fiction: "mini" Helen Van Slyke or Danielle Steele novels, not romantic fantasies or formula romance. We welcome a wide range of plots. The heroine should be 25 to 50 years old; the setting should be within the United States.

We prefer to see a complete manuscript, with a length of 50,000 to 100,000 words. Please enclose a short synopsis and a cover letter describing your writing background. The manuscript should be typed on one side of white paper and should be double-spaced. Please make sure your name and full mailing address and phone number appear on a cover page, and include a self-addressed, stamped envelope with your submission. We ask that you keep a copy of all material you submit.

We want strong mainstream writers, authors of special vision, unique "voice," and inexhaustible plot ideas. We look to develop each writer over many books. We believe in our authors.

E. P. DUTTON, INC.

Heavenly Romances

Kathy O'Hehir, Editor
E. P. Dutton, Inc.
2 Park Avenue
New York, New York 10016

Heavenly Romances is a line of contemporary romance novels for 12- to 16-year-old girls. They are stories of growing up, of sharing and discovering one's identity, while experiencing the joy and wonder of falling in love for the first time. They should depict young adulthood from the point of view of contemporary teens and will describe adolescence as the readers themselves experience it.

Plots for Heavenly Romances should deal with the day-to-day problems, concerns, fears, and joys of the heroine's first or early romantic encounter. The heroine is 15 or 16, and is a high school student; the hero is a year or two older. There is no explicit sex or profanity allowed, and the limits of romantic encounters should be kissing and feelings of attraction tastefully expressed.

The stories should be set in the United States only, generally at school, summer camp, dances, the movies, snack bars, or other wholesome settings or locales.

The books should run between 35,000 and 40,000 words, written for average to good readers. Submissions should consist of two sample chapters, a complete synopsis, and character descriptions.

All submissions will be acknowledged, provided that a postcard is enclosed, and, upon the author's request, rejected manuscripts will be returned, if postage is enclosed.

POCKET BOOKS

Tapestry Romances

Kate Duffy, Senior Editor
Pocket Books
1230 Avenue of the Americas
New York, New York 10020

Tapestry Romances are paperback originals, using an historical background. There is no restriction on geographical setting, but the novel should take place between 1066 and the late 19th century. The desired length for manuscripts is 85,000 words. Writers should query first, and include a synopsis and three sample chapters. Payment is made on an advance royalty basis.

The name *Tapestry* was chosen for its historical significance; long before women were taught to read and write, tapestries were used to record events and stories, especially the exploits of courageous knights and their ladies. Many tapestries have endured for hundreds of years, telling of an age and place far different from what we know today. "Tapestry" reflects the historical nature of the romance series and the uniqueness of each story.

ZONDERVAN CORPORATION

Serenade
Serenade/Saga

Ann W. Severance, Editor
Zondervan Corporation
749 Templeton Drive
Nashville, Tennessee 37205

The Serenade and The Serenade/Saga Series offer Christian readers good books characterized by intriguing story lines with no offensive speech, behavior, or philosophy. All elements of the books in these lines will reflect an evangelical world view with an emphasis on romantic love from the Christian perspective.

Writers should submit an annotated chapter outline, brief synopsis, biographical sketch, and sample chapter before submitting the complete manuscript. Payment is made on a royalty basis.

Serenade

Characters: The *heroine* should be a young woman between the ages of 24 and 35. She may be beautiful, merely attractive, or plain—with true beauty emerging as a result of inner resources and/or love that literally transforms her outward appearance. She may be wholesomely seductive, with an inherent, but unpracticed, sensuality. In keeping with contemporary lifestyles, she would probably be a working girl. The heroine may or may not be a Christian at the outset. If not, however, she must be profoundly and positively affected by the Christian values of some other character, probably the hero.

The *hero* should be strong and assertive, a combination of the "tough and tender" personality admired by many women. Professionally, he could be anything from a businessman to a wealthy playboy who later "reforms," from a clergyman to a blue-collar worker. To allow for glamorous and exotic settings, however, at least one of the protagonists should be affluent, with the wealth derived from inheritance or earning power.

Secondary characters: While the main action of the plot must revolve around the two leading characters, minor characters are important in providing complication: *i.e.,* the "other woman or man" who vies for the affections of the hero or heroine; a clinging parent; dependent siblings, etc. These secondary characters can be quite vividly portrayed and are necessary to the development of the plot.

Setting: The locale might be any city, town, or rural community in the United States, but an international setting is acceptable as long as the main characters are American. Surroundings, whatever the location, should be conducive to romance and intimacy—candlelight, firelight, music, fine foods, cruise ships, etc.

Plot: A simple love story, expertly told, can be deeply moving and inspirational. A series of complicating factors, either physical (external) or spiritual (internal), must ensue before a resolution is reached, culminating in a *happy ending.* All references to Christianity should be a natural outgrowth of plot and characters.

Treatment of Potentially Sexual Scenes: In this genre, there will be inevitable moments of sexual tension between the lead characters. Descriptions of kissing and embracing are permitted within the bounds of good taste. The ability of the hero and/or heroine to observe certain limits—*i.e.,* prevent sexual feelings from overpowering them—is an essential distinction of the Christian romance. The difference between lust and love should also be noted.

Length: 50,000 to 55,000 words.

*   *   *

Serenade/Saga

Characters: The *heroine* should be a young woman between the ages of 17 and 30. She may be beautiful, merely attractive, or plain—with true beauty emerging as a result of inner resources and/or love that literally transforms her outward appearance. She may be wholesomely seductive, with an inherent, but unpracticed, sensuality.

According to the particular historical setting chosen by the author, this character would probably not be stereotypical of her age, breaking out of the prescribed "mold" with a strong sense of self and independent thought.

The *hero,* in his mid to late thirties or early forties, should portray the bold, assertive masculine characteristics necessary to the building of new frontiers. Tenderness and sensitivity may be latent, revealed only as the romantic relationship develops.

Secondary characters: While the main action of the plot must revolve around the two leading characters, minor characters are essential in providing complication: *i.e.,* the "other woman or man" who vies for the affections of the hero or heroine; a clinging parent; dependent siblings, etc. These secondary characters can be quite vividly portrayed and are necessary to the development of the plot.

Setting: The historical backdrop against which the action develops should be accurately described to the extent that the reader feels transported to another time and place. The time frame includes the founding of America (the United States and Canada) and the historical period up to the turn of the century (1900). The action, therefore, could take place on the frontier, in colonial New England or the picturesque Southland, in small villages or burgeoning towns, or even on shipboard, which would permit the local color of numerous ports of call. An international flavor may be introduced, if desired, with the narrative spanning the immigration of peoples from other countries and the subsequent settling by ethnic groups. The author should be well acquainted with the historical and geographical background of the chosen locale.

Plot: A simple love story, expertly told, can be deeply moving and inspirational. An added dimension inherent in this series might be an emphasis upon the strong spiritual and moral fiber which characterized many of the early settlers of this country, and the solidarity of the family unit. A series of complicating factors, either physical (external) or spiritual (internal), must ensue before a resolution is reached, culminating in a *happy ending.* All references to Christianity should be a natural outgrowth of plot and characterizations.

Treatment of Potentially Sexual Scenes: In this genre, there will be inevitable moments of sexual tension between the lead characters. Descriptions of kissing and embracing are permitted within the bounds of good taste. The ability of the hero and/or heroine to observe certain limits—*i.e.,* prevent sexual feelings from overpowering them—is an essential distinction of the Christian romance. The physical expression of love should be true to the social conventions of the era as well as to the Christian ethic. The difference between lust and love should also be noted.

Length: 50,000 to 55,000 words.

BANTAM BOOKS
Sweet Dreams

Eve Becker, Associate Editor
Cloverdale Press
133 Fifth Avenue
New York, NY 10003

Each Sweet Dreams romance features a heroine who is about sixteen years old—an ordinary, middle-class suburban girl, with a family to match. The romantic interest, a boy of the same age or a little older, should appear early in the story—the sooner the better. The girl should have a warm, supportive family, and one or two close friends in whom she confides. The plot is moved by a conflict or conflicts embracing adolescent life—finding one's identity, finding that special boy, choosing between suitors, overcoming shyness or self-doubt, becoming popular, succeeding in sports, and so forth. Variations in the above guidelines are acceptable if integral to the plot.

Characterization is paramount in Sweet Dreams. It should move the plot, rather than be dictated by it. Character motivation and personal growth are essential to all Sweet Dreams heroines.

Lastly, there should be no profanity, no religious references, and no explicit sex. We endorse hugging and kissing, of course. Where would romance be without them?

If you are interested in writing a Sweet Dreams romance, we welcome complete outlines and a sample chapter of your story. Also include any pertinent information about yourself and your writing experience.

AVON BOOKS

The Avon Romance

Page Cuddy, Editorial Director
Avon Books
1790 Broadway
New York, New York 10019

The Avon Romance is a showcase for new romance writers. We'll publish them (but never more than one a month) when we find new writers who seem to merit some special attention. They can be first novelists or simply new to Avon.

The Avon Romance can be either historical or contemporary, and should be approximately 100,000 words in length.

Basically, we are looking for what we've always looked for in the romance: good stories with vivid characters. We want books that writers feel they *have to write!*

*   *   *

Avon's Velvet Glove Romantic Suspense Series

Meredith G. Bernstein
Literary Agent
33 Riverside Drive
New York, New York 10023

Denise Marcil Literary Agency
316 West 82nd Street
New York, New York 10024

Concept: The Velvet Glove novel will represent an updated version of the romantic suspense novel in the tradition of Mary Stewart. The distinguishing feature of this line is its emphasis on sensuality. These novels are characterized by a sense of discovery on the part of the heroine. In solving the mystery, the protagonist will uncover something about herself (i.e., trusting her intuition; her ability to persevere; the benefits of her particular skills). These novels will feature an American heroine, set against any foreign or American background. They should have a page-turning quality with good pacing achieved by realistic complications, multiple settings, and sensual romance. Unlike this genre's forebears these books will have modern heroines who are passionate and sophisticated. The writer must create an equal balance of mystery and suspense with romance, any shift leaning in the direction of romance. Stories and characters must be believable for the contemporary reader. Avoid contrived situations; avoid actions of the characters based on misunderstandings or assumptions. The books, 60–65,000 words, are written in the third person.

Plot: An imaginative, contemporary plot relating to universal situations or dilemmas. Avoid obvious and familiar complications, i.e., smuggling (art, drugs, jewels). Resolution of plot should be upbeat; violence is not an element in this series. Again, the plot should be enriched by the skills and idiosyncrasies of the hero and heroine.

Heroine: Suggested age: between 25 and 35, American. The heroine can be any size or shape, and does not have to be physically perfect. She must, however, be attractive in her own way, and shine from within. She should be clever, quick-witted, generous of spirit, charming and with her own sense of style. She should have a specific interest or career that gives the reader some new knowledge about any given field. In other words, the background must contribute materially to the fabric of the suspense.

Unlike the classic gothic, our heroine is an active figure and she is never a "real" victim, e.g., an orphan, oppressed captive, at the mercy of anyone who controls her purse strings. In most instances where the heroine senses trouble, she does not become passive.

It would be desirable to endow the heroine with some memorable facet or ability, i.e., athletic prowess, a photographic memory, sense of humor, etc.

In order to underscore the sensual elements of this series, the heroines should be comfortable with and aware of themselves in terms of their sexuality.

Hero: Hero should be 25 to 35, any nationality. Like the heroine, he should be realistic and human. He's not the stereotypic tall, brawny, arrogant man and does not have to be classically handsome. Further, the hero should also have some particular talent or ability. He must be somewhat vulnerable or sensitive and exhibit some charm or sense of humor. Writers should aim for some realistic chemistry between the hero and heroine. The hero's role is not one of savior but rather soul-mate, team mate or support system for the heroine. Hero may be enigmatic, with the heroine uncertain of his intentions.

Setting: American or international setting may contribute to the story line in several ways and should be evoked realistically. For example, if the story were about evil doings at the Kentucky Derby, it would be necessary to develop realistic details of the race, of the political climate, of the "horse personnel" or the region. It is important to make the reader feel that she is there.

Submissions: Please send a query letter, including a short synopsis of story (3 to 5 pages) and first chapter (optional). Also enclose a short biographical note and a stamped, self-addressed envelope.

*   *   *

Avon's Finding Mr. Right

Meredith G. Bernstein
Literary Agent
33 Riverside Drive
New York, New York 10023

Denise Marcil Literary Agency
316 West 82nd Street
New York, New York 10024

We want full-length novels about contemporary life and love. Each of these should be filled with romance and adventure and feature a lively heroine faced with crucial choices about her career and love life. Though she may not find the 100% perfect man, she finds the man who is perfect for her.

Query, with synopsis, as indicated for the Velvet Glove series.

Additional Romance Lines

*It's a good idea to write to the editors for the latest information before submitting manuscripts.

Caprice—Ace Books, 200 Madison Avenue., New York, NY 10016.
 Contemporary romances for teen-agers, 40,000 to 45,000 words. Query with outline and self-addressed, stamped envelope. Pays on a royalty basis or by outright purchase.

Dream-Your-Own Romance Stories—Wanderer Books, Simon & Schuster, 1230 Ave. of the Americas, New York, NY 10020.
 Multiple plot romances for readers aged 8 and up. Submit complete manuscripts. Pays on royalty or flat fee basis.

Ecstasy Supreme—Candlelight Romances, Dell Publishing Co., 245 E. 47th St., New York, NY 10017. Anne Gisonny, Senior Editor.
 Highly sensual, contemporary adult romances, 85,000 to 100,000 words. Submit complete manuscript or a partial manuscript of at least 70 pages with a complete outline. Pays on royalty basis.

Follow Your Heart Romances—Archway Paperbacks, 1230 Ave. of the Americas, New York, NY 10020.
 Romances for girls grades 5 to 7, in multiple choice format. Submit summary or outline of the entire book, two or three complete tracks, and cover letter. Pays on royalty basis.

Scarlet Ribbons—New American Library, 1633 Broadway, New York, NY 10019.
 Fairly sexually explicit historical romances for adults, 125,000 to 150,000 words. Query. Pays on royalty or flat fee basis.

Starlight—Doubleday & Co., 245 Park Ave., New York, NY 10167.
Contemporary adult romances, 70,000 to 75,000 words. Send
complete manuscripts with outline. Pays on royalty basis.

Young Love—Dell Publishing Co., 245 E. 47th St., New York, NY
10017.
Contemporary romances for teens, in which the heroines are
at least 14 years old. Write for tip sheet. Pays on royalty basis.